The Chronicles
of a
Wanderer

by Joan Woodley

TRAFFORD

Canadian Cataloguing in Publication Data

Woodley, Joan, 1915-
    The chronicles of a wanderer

    ISBN 1-55212-512-2

    1. Woodley, Joan, 1915-   2. British Canadians--
Biography.* I. Title.
FC27.W66A3 2000   971'.0042'0092   C00-911327-4
F1034.3.266A3 2000

TRAFFORD

This book was published *on-demand* in cooperation with Trafford Publishing.
On-demand publishing is a unique process and service of making a book available
for retail sale to the public taking advantage of on-demand manufacturing and
Internet marketing.**On-demand publishing** includes promotions, retail sales,
manufacturing, order fulfilment, accounting and collecting royalties on behalf of
the author.
Suite 6E, 2333 Government St., Victoria, B.C. V8T 4P4, CANADA

Phone	250-383-6864	Toll-free	1-888-232-4444 (Canada & US)
Fax	250-383-6804	E-mail	sales@trafford.com
Web site	www.trafford.com		

Trafford Catalogue #00-0177   www.trafford.com/robots/00-0177.html

10   9   8   7   6

Acknowledgments

My work on this book commenced with my joining the Brock House Writers. I would like to thank Dr. Sydney Butler and Professor Emeritus Frank Bertram of the University of British Columbia, who conducted the classes. Their guidance and encouragement helped to unlock the memories and inspired me to write my life's story.

Dedication

Dedicated to my four children,
Barbara Ray, Graham, Jennefer
and Nick, and to my nephew
Shaun McAndrew.

Contents

Part One
England 1915–1948

SARRE: THE PLACE
WHERE I WAS BORN

☞

*I*t is hard to believe that Sarre was once a bustling seaport. But that was centuries ago, before the river dried up leaving just a little village in rural England, buried in the heart of Kent.

My home was on the edge of the marshes. I loved the marshes and would wander off with the dog. I can still see the wind blowing the grass till it shone. I did not know it then, but I was absorbing impressions, probably for the book that I did not know I would one day write.

Everywhere was safe in those days and my mother only had to look through the window to see where I was. It was flat marshland divided by dykes, with rushes rustling in the breeze and in summertime, bright yellow marsh marigolds like huge buttercups, flourished and reflected in the water, and skylarks sang as they lilted their way up – and – up into the air. Birds and sheep were my companions.

I remember the shepherd with his crook always after some wayward lamb. I was quite small but I think he liked me tagging along. Sometimes he gave me an orphaned lamb to feed from a bottle. I loved the smell of its little warm wriggling body and the rough feel of its woolly coat. The shep-

herd had a beautiful face wreathed in smiles and wrinkles
and when I grew older I photographed him with a lamb tucked
under his arm, then, enlarged and framed I gave it to him. He
was delighted and placed it above the fireplace in his thatched
cottage where it remains to this day, although he has long
since passed on.

Sarre was no larger than a hamlet, a rustic spot, without a church or school, or even a village green. The nearest
church was a mile away with its tall tower standing like a
guardian above the roofs and chimneys, and every Sunday
my sister and I walked with our father to morning service. I
would have been six or seven years old at the time, and my
sister two years older. We walked along the bridle path
through the cornfields, and when the service was over we
hurried home to mother, and Daniel, our little black and tan
terrier who were always there to welcome us.

Our home was Victorian large and rambling with a
pretty walled garden. Flower beds and fruit trees surrounded
the lawn and I remember especially the cosy winter evenings
with log fires, the soft glow of paraffin lamps and candles, the
candlesticks that were left on the hall table for us to carry
upstairs to the nursery at bedtime.

The village possessed a post office. It was the front room
of a private home belonging to my Grandmother, Elizabeth
Packham, who lived there with her son, my Uncle George.
There were two pubs: The Kings Head, a Victorian brick building with lawns and large elm trees where Devonshire teas
were served in the summertime, and it was rumoured in the
village that it was haunted, some even said they had seen the
ghost, "You watch out when the moon is full, that's when you

will see it!"

The other belonged to my Grandfather Loft. Above the entrance door the date 1666. It was known locally as the Cherry Brandy House and was famous for the cherry brandy made and sold there.

The Inn was halfway between London and Dover. My mother told stories about the stage-coaches pulled by a team of horses and used to carry passengers and mail. A recent discovery, just by the 'maids bedroom', on the top floor, a cobwebbed cranny full of dusty bric-a-brac came to light. The trove included fading visitors' books and hunting prints. A glance at the visitors books confirm that Rudyard Kipling, Lloyd George and Charlie Chaplin and many other film stars of the day stayed there. But the most celebrated guest, in my grandfather's time, was the Prince of Wales, later Edward VII, who presented my grandfather with a set of six silver forks, each fork engraved with the Prince of Wales feathers. It was at this Inn that my parents met... and fell in love. They were married in 1911.

Many years later I did a nostalgic trip into the past and revisited Sarre. The house where I was born had not changed externally but it had been converted into two homes. The staid Kings Head of yester-year still served Devonshire teas in the summertime and the ghost of ill-repute continued to move chairs around in the night, or so it was said!

Time had not changed the Cherry Brandy House. The timeless 17th century building had endured two wars. It had been updated to modern day standards and had retained its old world elegance and charm. The room overlooking the tea gardens dedicated to the novelist, Charles Dickens who wrote some of his novels there remained. The cobble-stones and stables where once the horses were groomed and rested, had been converted into gardens and modern suits for the guests.

But gone were my beloved marshes! The serenity and atmosphere of peace remained but the green pastoral setting had given way to arable land and cornfields, stretching in seemingly endless waves of gold into the distance while Sarre, still remained a little speck on the map... one of God's treasures.

LIFE IN A CONVENT

☙

I shall always remember my mother taking me to school for the very first time – her footsteps echoing down the lofty hall, the heavy oak door and the bolt being drawn as my mother was leaving. I felt so very small and alone amidst the statues on the walls and Our Lord looking down upon me.

But that day I met two new girls who were small like me. When the lunchtime bell rang we took our sandwiches into the lovely gardens and sat on the lawns under the trees. That was the beginning of our lasting friendships. Later we were to become inseparable. We went everywhere together enjoying the same interests, all of us liking the same sports, roaming the countryside, camping and hiking. Our formative years were happy years.

When we were about ten years old we became boarders together. Life in the convent was very different to what we had been accustomed – we lost our freedom.

The nuns on the whole were kind and discipline was strict, not unusual in those days. Everything was done by the school bell, from getting up in the morning, washing, dressing, making our beds, and getting to chapel on time for prayers, and lining up in orderly fashion before going into the diningroom for breakfast. Talking was forbidden until grace was said. When the meal was over the bell silenced us again. We filed quietly to the change room outside and donned our sports gear. Then followed a half hour of physical exercises before changing back into our uniforms and lining up for our respective class rooms and the daily grind of learning.

We had a good education, I think, although I was not academically inclined and won no awards other than a silver cup for tennis and some medals for sport. I sang in the school choir and took an active part in the end of year school concerts when our parents and friends filled the hall and listened with great pride as we all performed.

Catholicism was taught daily. The non-catholics had readings from the Bible, and in all fairness to the nuns, they at no time tried to convert us.

The ritual of the regular baths remains a vivid memory. We had to wear brown calico shifts in the water so as not to appear before ourselves in the nude.

On one memorable occasion I was caught flinging a pillow at one of the girls just as a nun was coming into the dormitory. It missed the girl and hit the nun on the side of her head knocking her veil askew. I think her anger was due, in part, to her shaven head being displayed for all the girls to see. I was made to dress and report to the Reverend Mother who was a person to be feared. She threatened me with expulsion but as I had previously maintained a good record, my punishment was to get up early before the others, and go to Mass and confess my sins. During the period of kneeling in repentance we had to keep our arms outspread. If we allowed them to rest on the pew behind, there was always a nun to gently raise them up. It was the punishment we most dreaded.

While I was still at school, three things happened that sent ripples of excitement through the girls:

I was still a junior when one of the senior girls left to join the Order. Her mother came to take her away and I could not understand how they both could look so happy. I felt devastated for them. How would my mother have felt if it had been me? Would she have been pleased or would she have tried to dissuade me in the hope that I would have changed my mind. I was young and the thought of being separated from my parents was unthinkable.

Then there was the nun, Sister St. Lelia, a beautiful woman. Even in her black habit she looked regal and dignified. She had a rich voice and taught us to sing, carrying us through our scales and arpeggios, psalms and anthems. We all loved her and it was a sad day for us when she renounced her vows and returned to her childhood sweetheart.

Sometime afterwards there were whispers among the girls of things that I did not understand – The convent was a teaching school and many young trainees passed through its doors. We liked these women and one in particular we loved. Her name was Josie. Josie was athletic and played a good game of tennis, and an aggressive game of hockey.

One day while we were playing tennis on our lunch break, the Reverend Mother sent for her. Josie pulled a wry face at us and walked towards the office. We never saw her again. She had been dismissed.

Why? What could she have done we all asked each other? It was a long time after the event that we learned the reason… she was a lesbian.

When I finally left school it was with a sense of relief.

Thank God, it is all over, I thought. But even then I could not reconcile myself with the idea and continued to return to the convent once a week to prolong my music studies. At the same time I completed a commercial course.

As for the three of us who met for the first time so long ago we rarely hear from each other now. We lost touch during the war and when it was over we were married and spread all over the globe, from England to Nairobi, and Australia.

ADOLESCENCE –
THE ROMANTIC YEARS

�

I don't remember my developing years, nor was I particularly interested. Sex was not talked about at home. It was very Victorian in that respect and when I asked my mother where babies came from, she said, "You will find out when you are old enough!" And that was that!

I slipped in and out of love, which brought many highs and lows. I remember being madly religious during that time and fantasized about becoming a missionary and going to Africa and converting the world. But my parents would have none of it and I had to content myself with playing the church organ. A dear soul, Miss Wiles, would pump the bellows while I played fugues and soulful dirges that transcended my woeful broken dreams.

It was about that time I met Francis. I was thirteen and he was fifteen, and I think he helped me over the difficult years. He made me a flower press. Together we roamed the marshes and woods, collecting specimens which we later researched. When I visited him in London where he lived, we hopped the double-decker buses, which were open on top, and I was introduced to the sights, museums and art galleries. As I look back, I think our meeting was designed by Francis's mother, and my mother who were 'old' school friends. If our organized meeting was intended to make me forget my religious zeal, it certainly succeeded – I thought I was in love! Until, I met David at a village hop. We met in a Paul Jones. When the music stopped we looked at one another for a brief moment, then he swept me off my feet and we danced the evening away.

We enjoyed other such evenings, and on one memorable occasion we borrowed two horses from one of the local farmers and rode over the marshes to the coast and along the water's edge, an exhilarating experience, and neither of us knew at the time that we would never see each other again.

When I did not hear from David I became anxious, until the postman eventually brought me a letter confirming what I suspected. He was at a nearby boarding school and had climbed through the cellar window to see me, and after our euphoric ride, he had been caught by the Headmaster and immediately sent home to face the wrath of his father.

"FOOTFALLS ECHO IN THE MEMORY"

❦

"Footfalls echo in the memory" — *T.S. Eliot*

$\mathcal{W}$hen I was young I spent many a holiday with an aunt of mine in Stalbridge, a little village in the heart of Dorset. English villages are noted for their air of timelessness and charm. I grew up in one. I loved them then, I love them now. We were taught to go to church regularly. That was a part of village life and when the service was over and we grew older, we would drop into the local pub for a drink, or simply visit friends, and by the time we reached home the roast beef and Yorkshire pudding would be cooked to a turn.

We had all been to church that Sunday. We went to the Anglican church, afterwards visiting friends of my aunt and uncle. I had met them and their son before, but I had not met the son's friend who was visiting from Oxford.

He was not very tall, just average. He had a crop of dark curly hair and a beautiful speaking voice. I was most impressed. But they were Methodists! Did it really matter? My aunt said, "They are different, dear." Well, different or not I was delighted when he invited me to go for a walk with him. It was summertime. The evenings were long and as darkness began to fall the birds were hushed, and the hedgerows seemed to come alive with the tiny lights of the glow-worms. We tried to touch these little lights which were never where they appeared to be, but our hands touched, and in the silence of the summer's evening we had our first embrace.

Harry was a most agreeable companion. He told me of his early life at Mill Hill, and later at Oxford, and what he hoped to achieve. He was studying history and music. Cricket was his hobby. We saw a lot of each other, every day going off somewhere on borrowed bikes and taking picnic lunches, cycling through country lanes and onto the moors, or walking through the gorse and sliding and scrambling down the tracks and trails to the beach below and finding some sheltered cove where we wouldn't be disturbed. I was so in love, I couldn't wait for each new day to unfold so we could spend every minute of our time together.

Before Harry left Oxford he invited me to a Ball where we danced the night away to the strains of Billy Cotton's Dance Band. It was June, and I recall the wisteria climbing over the ancient walls of the colleges – lilac, purple and white blossoms carried on the breeze like confetti. We danced out-of-doors on the lawns under the trees... so long ago. I wore a pale, leaf-green chiffon dress, I remember. And yet... sometimes it seems like yesterday that we stood together and watched as daylight broke and Oxford was bathed in sunrise turning the magnificent church spires into a city aglow.

We punted our way up the river between the weeping willows to the Copper Kettle, a 17th century restaurant for breakfast. We drank mead amidst the brasses and low beams, and sat on the dark old oaken settles... just musing, and enjoying each other until Harry had to return to the university and my future-in-laws came to take me home. My happiness was complete in the knowledge that Harry and I would one day be married.

⋐ ⋐ ⋐ ⋐ ⋐ ⋐ ⋐

Years later I was searching for his photograph, I knew I had it somewhere in amongst my treasures. When I found it I touched it lovingly and looked at the man before me. We were in Bournemouth walking along the promenade, celebrating our engagement. As I sat there I had a curious feeling that he was in the room and reached out to touch him. "Oh, Harry dear!" I said aloud, "if only"... but he had already disappeared into the mists of time leaving a sense of sorrow and loneliness for what might have been. Harry was killed in action in 1940.

NO WAY OF KNOWING

❧

 $\mathcal{M}$ y sister, Molly, and I, were vacationing in Switzerland. It was the summer of 1938. We had crossed the English Channel, and on reaching France we went by train. My memory is hazy about that part of the journey. However, I do recall being given pillows for a few cents apiece on which to rest our heads, for it was a night's journey through Europe to Switzerland.

When we reached Vitznau it was early morning. We had crossed Lake Lucerne by ferry to the terminus at the foot of the steps leading to our hotel, which was tucked into the foothills of the Rigi. We disembarked and were hauled up by two stalwart men and taken the rest of the way. Here we were greeted with friendly smiles and shown into the dining-room. The gorgeous aroma of hot coffee filled us with delight. The dining-room jutted out over the lake, the water was blue, the early morning sunlight pale and low, and all around us were mountains, and more mountains, all covered in snow. We could not wait to don our boots! As soon as breakfast was over, without even unpacking, we set off to explore the foot-hills, such was the exuberance of youth.

Our entire holiday was an active one. We hiked mostly, rowed on the lake, danced in the beer gardens nightly. The beer gardens were small circular areas, smooth like marble, and the dances consisted mainly of waltzes played at a rapid tempo to the accompaniment of a piano accordion, a violin and some small drums. My feet hardly seemed to touch the ground: I was light-headed. It was a new and novel experience and the music set my pulse racing.

We visited Basel, a city in Northern Switzerland, and after wandering through the cathedral and art galleries we stopped for a drink and sat beside the River Rhine and waited for the ferry to take us back to Vitznau. As we stepped aboard I saw a man looking at me: he was tall and elegantly dressed.

We smiled at each other and chatted as we crossed Lake Lucerne.

"I live in Brussels,"he said, "and am visiting Switzerland. I'm presently staying in Vitznau." He spoke perfect English and when I told him that we, too, were staying in Vitznau, he was pleased.

"Let's dance tonight in the beer gardens!" he said.

After dinner Molly and I wandered along. The music was playing and Paul was waiting. We swung into the rhythm, and Molly met Ernst who was German. The four of us became friendly and spent many hours hiking together. Language was no barrier as we found almost everyone we met along the way spoke French, German and English.

One day we set off to climb the Rigi. We didn't reach the summit, neither did we aspire to such heights. We stopped often, picking berries and gazing into the valleys below where there were usually a cluster of chalets and peasant women, sometimes sitting outside their front doors, or in the narrow streets on hard wooden seats, making lace of the most exquisite kind. And always the sound of the cowbells echoing through the hills.

It took us many hours to climb the Rigi's mountain peaks. We climbed higher and higher, and as we were sitting beside the edge of a cliff overlooking the valley and enjoying our pack lunch, I was surprised to hear thunder and remarked on it to Paul. He said it was an avalanche, and almost immediately a mass of snow roared down the mountainside in front of where we were sitting and into the valley below. Then all was hushed.

From Vitznau the four of us moved on to Wengen. Vitznau was small and filled with charm with its mountains, pretty lake-side chalets, and window boxes asplash with colour and serenity. By contrast, Wengen was larger but still no more than a village overlooking the beautiful Lauterbrunen Valley, dominated by the majestic Jungfrau. The air was intoxicating. We seemed to climb forever by day. In the evenings the music called us back to dance until the orchestra ceased to play and the stars looked down upon us as we made our way back to our hotel. How happy we all were during that lovely summer of 1938.

The chamois and the ibex lived high in the mountains and we followed their trails to a farm house. On the door was a sign offering refreshments for the weary. There we ate wild strawberry tarts and drank iced goats milk. Why it was all so delicious and has remained in my memory, I do not know. Maybe it was the company we were with, or the clouds slipping in and out of the mountain peaks, the sun glistening on the snow, or the immensity and infinite peace and beauty of our surroundings. And as the clouds slipped in and out of the mountain peaks, so the clouds of war gathered which would soon envelop all our lives, never to be the same again.

Our holiday almost at an end, everything and everywhere became especially precious as we climbed the Jungfrau for the last time. We gathered the tiny, velvety-white edelweiss blossoms that grew on the mountain slopes, and which we later gave to each other as little expressions of love and happiness. Before we parted Paul gave me a wooden carving of a Swiss bear. I still have it and with the passage of time, it remains one of life's cherished memories.

What became of those two young men, so young, so vibrant, so full of hope, I will never know. I like to believe that the edelweiss I gave Paul kept him safe, but I have no way of knowing because all communication ceased when the German army invaded Belgium in 1940.

THANET HOUSE

❧

*W*hen I left school, I did not know what I wanted to do. I had not been an industrious student or studied seriously. I had worked slavishly at the subjects I liked and was passionate about sport. As a child, I had climbed trees and run wild with my brother. It seemed logical to me that I would become a Physical Fitness instructor, but when I mentioned it to my mother the idea was greeted with a blunt rebuffal. "You are tomboy enough!" I accepted her advice and pursued a commercial course during my last year at school.

Sometime later, my sister Molly, and I, together with Dorothy, a friend, were looking through the job vacancies in the local paper when I observed an advertisement and pointed it out to Molly. I suggested she apply. Dorothy turned to me and said, "why don't you?" I thought about it and decided to take the plunge.

The advertisement was for a secretary in a boys' preparatory school, Thanet House, situated in Westgate on the Kent coast, only a half -hour's bus ride from home.

The Headmaster, Dr. Paul Murphy, was a tall blue-eyed Scot, his partner, the Reverend Jefferson. I was interviewed by both these men. I remember being very nervous but when I left the school, and was walking up the drive to catch my bus home, it was with a feeling of jubilation. I had my first job, and as it transpired, it was also my last. I commenced at the beginning of the school year, September 1936.

It was a small boarding school of about eighty boys, many of them sons of old boys. There were masters of all ages, young and middle aged, and a music teacher, the only woman on the teaching staff. She taught pianoforte and violin, and trained the choir. There was a resident matron and nurse as well as a visiting physician, an excellent cook, kitchen staff, Norman the odd-job man, and gardeners.

The grounds were extensive with rose gardens, herbaceous beds and playing fields. The main sports were cricket, rugby and soccer, but emphasis was on academic subjects. At a young age the boys sat their Common Entrance examinations for Eton, Harrow, and Sandhurst if they were going into the Military Academy, or whichever public school their fathers had attended.

My routine was always the same. Immediately after assembly, Dr. Murphy dictated his letters, and the Reverend Jefferson dictated sermons and lectures. I then retired to my office and typed, sorted the daily mail, and kept the accounts up to date.

It was a happy school with a good chapel for Sunday worship when Mary accompanied the choir, and if I was on duty I filled in. This was followed by a walk, all the boys two-by-two. There was discipline then. Everything seemed peaceful, as if it could last forever.

At the end of each term when all the boys had been sent home and the final accounts posted, I, too, was free, and that was a bonus for me. I saved my salary, and in 1938 I went to Switzerland for my first holiday beyond England.

I was fascinated by language and the fluent use of English, French and German, and as Thanet House was situated next to a convent I called to see the Reverend Mother. I explained that I wanted to improve my French and wondered if I could have some private tuition. The Reverend Mother introduced me to a French nun. We became friendly during my weekly visits, and towards the end of the year she asked me if I would like to stay with her family in Paris. My parents thought it an experience not to be missed.

"Possibly your last opportunity to visit Europe," my father said.

Plans were made. I was to be wearing a red scarf, so also was my hostess. This was our identification.

My mother came to Dover to see me off. Waving frantically and promising to write often, I sailed away into the unknown. I crossed the English Channel by steamer and took the metro to Paris where I was met by Babette and her mother, Madame de la Crochais, all three of us waving a red scarf.

When we reached their home I was introduced to the three adult sons and Monsieur, a parliamentarian, a worried man who feared war was unavoidable. My task was to converse in English with Babette, an attractive, sophisticated young woman of sixteen.

It was bitterly cold that winter but Babette and I used to wrap up in our overcoats and boots and walk along the banks of the River Seine. I learned to eat snails and became accustomed to garlic, and wine with every meal.

Christmas Day we were invited to the home of relatives. We sat round the fire and talked. The food was sumptuous, the coloured lights and Christmas decorations gay, but it was overshadowed by the conversation which inevitably turned to thoughts of war that was uppermost in everyone's mind.

New Year's Eve Madame de la Crochais was gay and excited.

"We mustn't let Hitler spoil the evening, must we?" she said. Monsieur shook his head sadly.

The furniture was removed from the hall, the rugs rolled up and taken away and the floor polished until it shone. A quartet was hired and by the time the guests began to arrive Babette could hardly contain her emotions. Pierre, her brother, was bringing along a friend whom Babette had met once before and had fallen in love. Both these young men were in the regular army.

The evening was electrified with gaiety. Babette looked radiant and vibrant in blue. I wore a black and gold lamé dress. Those were the days of elegance when women wore long dresses and men wore dinner jackets. There were many young people there and we danced the evening away. At midnight we all toasted each other with champagne, and when the church bells rang to welcome in the New Year Monsieur wept as he said, "Vive la France!" None of us could have imagined that nine months later Britain and France would be at war with Germany.

I returned home and to Thanet House. On the surface everything appeared unchanged, but one by one the young masters volunteered and I found myself drawn into teaching. The parents wrote concerned for their sons' safety, and evacuation was considered.

Night after night we listened to the evening news broad-
casts on the wireless as Hitler established military conscrip-
tion and created the Luftwaffe.

We found a mansion in the heart of Herefordshire that
solved the problem. Preparations were made to leave the Kent
coast. We piled into buses and as we drove away the Royal
Air Force commandeered the building and began moving in.

The veterans of the first World War came with us together with the cook and the matron, while the domestic staff
left to join up.

The building we were renting was the perfect place for
all the boys. The grounds were large and the surrounding
countryside glorious with woods filled with bracken and birch
trees. No longer were there sports teams but the boys were
taken for an early morning run each day, and there were
picnics.

It was peaceful there, but it was a false calm. Hitler
seized Austria and Czechoslovakia. The British Prime Minis-
ter conferred with Hitler and Mussolini in Munich. It was
known as the Munich Agreement. When Neville Chamber-
lain returned triumphant to London waving a bit of paper in
his hand, he said, "The pact which I have signed means peace
in our time."

But Hitler violated every treaty and September 1st, 1939
his troops smashed into Poland. Two days later, September
3rd, Britain and France declared war on Germany.

The strain weighed heavily on the Doctor. He had four
sons of military age. One morning during assembly he rose to
speak to the boys, and as he did so, he put his hand to his
chest and slumped to the floor.

Everyone had loved their headmaster. A cloud of sorrow hovered over us, the boys' constant chatter was silenced as they spoke quietly amongst each other and wondered what would happen to them.

I stayed and helped Mrs. Murphy with the final letters and reports. Many of the boys' parents were in India which was still a British colony and alternative accommodation had to be found for them. The boys were resilient and after a while the thought of going home excited them. "No more school" they all chanted as they waited for their parents to come and take them home.

The huge mansion we were renting was strangely silent after everyone had left and Mrs. Murphy and I were glad to close the heavy oak doors for the last time. Thanet House as we had known it, was finished. It was the end of an era.

THE DAYS IN BETWEEN

❧

I had been so engrossed with the closing of the school that I had given little heed to Hitler and his planned invasion of Britain. But now the time had come for me to leave and return to my family in Kent.

I caught the train home. My mother and father welcomed me and I was delighted to be with them again. We talked well into the night and I soon realized anything could happen.

The Battle of Britain was just beginning. The quiet village I had known had changed out of all recognition. It was bustling with military, gun emplacements, trenches, and the fields were a network of barbed wire. The boys' college, and the childrens' hospital had been evacuated and requisitioned by the army, and there was an almost total absence of civilians.

My brother and sister had joined up: Eric in the Royal Air Force, and Molly in the WAAF. I promptly enlisted. Once accepted I was impatient to be off. The raids were heavy as night after night Hitler systematically bombed air fields and factories, and dog fights were a daily occurrence.

The last day of 1940 had been quiet and free from raids. We had walked over the marshes in the morning while the sun glimmered feebly through the winter clouds. In the evening we joined our neighbours, the Shaws, for cards, and at midnight we drank to peace, and a speedy end to the war. At home we kissed each other good-night and after one final hug we went to bed.

I don't know what time it was when my father came to my room and sat on my bed. He put his head in his hands. I thought he was ill.

"Father, are you alright?" I asked.

"Mother has just died," he said.

I rushed to her in disbelief. I was so shocked, momentarily I felt nothing. I kissed her, she was still warm, only 54, much too young to die. With my father's arm round me and without a word we went into the kitchen where there was always warmth from an anthracite stove in the corner of the room. My father struck a match and lit the old fashioned gas mantle and automatically I put the kettle on. We looked at each other in silence. My father had faith: he was a good man and believed in life eternal.

'In the midst of life we are in death', I thought. 'What, I wonder, does happen to us afterwards'?

Life was never quite the same again. Our mother had suffered an aneurysm. Her devastating sudden and unexpected death was indescribable. The responsibility of running the home now fell on my shoulders and all hope and thought of joining-up ended for me that night: I could not leave my father.

I helped in the business and became a Warden. Day and night we did four hourly shifts and kept vigil from the church tower. From our vantage point, looking across the

English Channel to the French coast we watched... and waited for the invasion that we all feared and expected.

At the height of the blitz on London day and night was filled with battles in the air. Kent became a battleground and the sirens became a familiar sound, aerodromes, shipping and the coastal towns were attacked. Dover, only a few minutes flying time from our village was heavily bombed. We watched from the church tower and in the event of invasion we would have rung the church bells. Mercifully that did not happen and we only learned, long afterwards, that Hitler commanded that Dover Castle be spared: that was where he planned his first meal when he set foot on English soil.

We became accustomed to the sirens and to the drone of bombers flying overhead. Dog-fights were a daily occurence when our Spitfires attacked their Messerschmitts. Shrapnel had to be raked from the lawns before we could cut them, and our roofs were pitted with holes where bits of the shells had fallen.

One night there was a huge explosion. We lost our windows and roof and enormous cracks appeared in the walls but the foundations remained strong and the noise from our ack ack guns was horrendous. I was waiting to go on nightshift when my bed was flung across the room and everything seemed to fall in around me. I rushed to my father who was lying there looking up into the stars.

"Phew," he said, "that was close!"

"Why aren't you in the shelter?" I asked.

"If I am going to be bombed I am going to be bombed in comfort," was his reply. I kissed him and loved him for his courage, he was a survivor, he would be alright.

BEQUET, AND THE CHANNEL ISLANDS

☙

*M*y mother and I had visited the Channel Islands a number of times before the war. We went by sea, or by air and stayed in St. Helier, the capital of Jersey. From there we visited the smaller islands of Guernsey and Sark. It was an enjoyable experience. The sun always seemed to shine and in June, our chosen month. it was perfect weather for swimming, picnicking, walking and scrambling over the rocks and beaches.

Because I had such happy memories of the islands I was interested in Bequet when we met one evening in the Bell Inn. Bequet was a Channel Islander and he liked to talk about his birth-place. He told me that the islands were largely self-governing and not bound by any Acts of Parliament even though they were a part of Britain. They had their own currency and paid little, or no taxes. He showed me photographs of the family home in St. Brelades Bay. They kept cattle, mostly Jersey and Guernsey cows. He talked about his early life and how happy he and his sister had been. He was sent to boarding school in England before finishing his education in France, and his father taught him the art of sailing. Soon after the declaration of war the Germans occupied the Channel Islands.

Bequet had joined the Army and was sent to England.

He was stationed in our village and thought it the most awful place on God's earth. But he didn't know it as I had known it before the war – the song of the blackbirds, song-thrushes and skylarks, sheep grazing on the marshes and golden corn in the summertime. Now the village was devoid of children and it resembled an army barracks equipped for war – trenches and barbed wire covered the fields and the heavy tread of the soldiers always on the march and waiting for the inevitable. Now only a sprinkling of civilians remained: Land Army girls and farm labourers worked the land, others ran the businesses and pubs and the vicar buried the dead and officiated at the communion and other services.

The troops spent time in the pubs. There they found warmth and comfort and after a drink or two, they forgot their woes and sang, Roll out the Barrel, and There'll always be an England, and several rather more scurrilous ditties, and at closing time the singing continued all the way back to their billets.

But that day we had been free of raids. It was a perfect cloudless summers day. I wandered to the Bell Inn where I knew Bequet would be waiting. He was talking with a group of men. I studied him: he was a dear man, moderately tall, strong build with large hands, he smiled often but rarely laughed. When he saw me he left the others and walked towards me. The sight of him filled me with warmth.

"Let's go outside," he said," it is getting noisy in here." He took my arm and we wandered down the lane that led to a farmhouse. It was quiet there. We scrambled on to a five-barred gate – he was very serious.

Suddenly, he said, "Will you marry me?"

I had lost my Harry, but you can't grieve forever and, of course, I said, "Yes, I would love to marry you."

Bequet told me that after our first meeting he felt less homesick and he hoped the farm would still be there when the war was over. He was longing to take me sailing and for me to meet his family. Then our peace was shattered by the wailing of the sirens and Bequet had to rush back to camp and I went hurriedly home. My emotions were high – I felt joyous, I also felt a deep foreboding.

Rumours began to circulate. Talk of being sent across the English Channel was on everyone's mind. The route marches intensified and the time came for them to pack up and move on. Bequet and I went for our last walk together. We promised to love each other always and to write often. We kept that promise. Then came the final leave. We rushed into each other's arms. We were overcome with a sense of finality that so many others were feeling but never voicing: would we ever see each other again? It was a question we asked ourselves, but never asked each other.

The weeks went by and my anxiety increased. When the telegram came as I knew it would, I wandered alone in the garden. The solace that I sought eluded me and I wondered how many more young men would have to die before life returned to normal, or if it ever would. Poor, dear Bequet.

A NEW BEGINNING

❧

*J*ohn was stationed in our village. He was attached to the Oxfordshire and Buckinghamshire regiment, the Ox and Bucks.

There was a dance in the village hall that evening. I went along with two young women who had joined the Land Army.

It was a fun evening and when the dance ended, John Woodley escorted me home. I invited him in for a drink. Once inside our livingroom his first words were, "Ah, a piano!" While I prepared the drinks John played, and to my amazement he could play anything by ear. I enjoyed listening and when he returned from his next leave he brought with him his violin and whenever there was a spare moment we relaxed and played duets together. Sometimes we wandered over the marshes and the little brick bridges that criss-crossed the dykes where we sat and talked and got to know each other. We were on double summertime and as the sun set, the moon rose and the daylight hours seemed unending: it was a beautiful summer that year of 1942.

Our courtship was short and we honeymooned briefly in a pub on the banks of the River Thames before John returned to his Regiment in Yorkshire, and I returned to my father.

One year later, Barbara Ray, our little daughter was born. She was born in an air raid. I remember watching the tracer bullets and listening to the bombs falling. I also remember thinking, "why aren't I afraid?" No one came to see if I was alright. I had waited nine months. Never before had I seen a new born baby. She was so small. I sat up and looked at her. Almost afraid to touch her I picked her up and held her close. I was oblivious to the raid and when the doctor eventually arrived and found us still attached, he smiled benignly at me and said, "Oh, you should have dozens!"

It was almost two years later that all leave was cancelled. A modicum of news filtered through the BBC, news of commando raids in Europe, tugs and gliders and paratroopers constantly on the move. There was an intensity in the air that had not been felt before. Eleanor, a friend, lived in a nearby village, she had cycled up the hill to visit me. We stood on the front lawn of my father's home and watched as hundreds of gliders filled the sky and flew towards the English Channel.

Eleanor looked at me and said, "I think it is the real thing, don't you?"

"It looks like it," I replied.

We spoke in hushed tones and were afraid.

We went inside and I put the kettle on. A sombre air overshadowed us. Eleanor's brother was in Auschwitz concentration camp. Eric, my brother was with Bomber Command, and John with the Royal Army Medical Corp. Paratroopers went ahead of the invasion forces, gliders took in men, jeeps, light artillery, and small tanks. Allied warships bombarded the coast. It was D-Day, June 6 1944: the beginning of the end of the war in Europe.

When war in Europe finally ended there was a sudden lull. As darkness settled over the countryside I went to draw the blackout and as I started to pull the curtains, I thought, "I don't need to do this now." My father came in at that moment and said, "I think you should, just in case." So for the last time the blackout curtains were drawn.

Although the war in Europe had ended we still had Japan to contend with. It was not until August 1945 when the Americans dropped the first atomic bomb on Hiroshima, and three days later a second larger atomic bomb fell on Nagasaki that the Japanese leaders surrendered. The agreement was signed aboard the American battleship *USS Missouri*, anchored in Tokyo Bay: September 2.

When John was demobilized we set about picking up the bits and pieces of our lives. John returned to his hospital in London to study anaestheology and, our little son was born – Graham John.

England was tired after the war. Young people with families were eager to leave, get away from it all and make a fresh start. John talked about emigrating to Canada, but in London he had met Jim Peters, a surgeon from Melbourne who persuaded John that Australia was a good country in which to bring up a family.

The idea did not appeal to me. I was reluctant to leave my father. But John wasted no time. He searched the advertisements and shipping agencies and in May, 1948 he sailed away as ship's surgeon on a cargo boat. He was paid a token wage of one shilling a week and free passage.

John liked Australia. He found accommodation and

wrote glowing letters of the sunshine, the shops filled with produce, "an abundance of everything," he said, while we, in England continued to grapple with rationing and coupon books that lasted for many years after the war ended.

Following John's example I went to London and harrassed the shipping agents, but without success. It soon became evident that there were simply not enough ships to carry the exodus of families waiting to go to Canada, Australia and New Zealand. I began to wonder if we would ever get away when I heard about Kearsley's Worldwide Travel. I rang them, I visited them, but it was always the same: there were long waiting lists. To fly to Australia we needed typhoid, smallpox and cholera inoculations, signed by the doctor and countersigned by our Medical Officer of Health. This was time consuming and a painful experience especially for the children. Finally, I received a letter from Kearsley's, written November 26, 1948 confirming our flight from London to Sydney. It would take five days.

The days leading up to our departure were harrowing. Our woes compounded by a thick fog that enveloped the whole of southern England. Several days passed and the weather showed no sign of improving. The air became still and silent. Everything was muffled, nothing stirred and an eeriness clung to us. I stood in the garden. I held out my arm and watched my hand disappear into the opaque nothingness.

Flights in and out of London were cancelled and we lived in a constant state of uncertainty. When the telephone call finally came we had little notice.

The thought of leaving my father weighed heavily on me, and how we all got away I will never know. My father came to London with us. We took a taxi from St Nicholas-at-Wade to Birchington-on-sea, a distance of three miles, and caught the steam train to Victoria Station. We chugged our way slowly through the fog and frequently stopped while the stoker walked along the tracks swinging a lantern to guide us.

Sandy, a good friend, lived in London. She had had the presence of mind to pick up my passport and meet us at Victoria Station.

We stayed at the Grosvenor Hotel where I was relieved to find our air tickets had been delivered. Gwendoline and Sydney, my aunt and uncle, were waiting for us, and Sandy stayed. We were a forlorn little group.

My father said, "When you are settled, I will join you in Australia."

I couldn't speak. I knew he never would.

We said our good-byes and I put the children to bed.

In the early hours of the morning we had a wake up call. Hurriedly I dressed myself before waking the children and the bus took us to the airport. It was still dark and the fog seemed thicker than ever.

Once the formalities of checking our tickets and baggage were over I took Ray by the hand and with Graham in my arms, we climbed into the plane. Our flight was the first to leave England in many days and in only a few short minutes we had risen above the fog and into the sunshine. A new beginning lay ahead of us. Ray sat beside me, and Graham sat on my lap. We looked through the window of the BO. 704/1 as we sped away and my last recollection of England was a country immersed in a gigantic pall of grey fog.

With mixed emotions I thought of my father, and all

that we were leaving behind... the home where I had spent
most of my life with its orchard and kitchen garden, the tennis court that had been such fun before the war, and the view

Telephone: WHitehall 7642 (10 lines)   Directors: J. W. Kearsley (Managing) F. E. Kearsley C. H. Cooper

J. W. KEARSLEY & CO., LTD.

CRAIG'S COURT HOUSE, 25 WHITEHALL, LONDON, S.W.I.

adjoining Trafalgar Square   Telegrams: Oceandair Parl London   Cables: Oceandair London   Codes: Bentley's Phrase

AIRWAYS & SHIPPING AGENTS   WORLD-WIDE TRAVEL & TRANSPORTATION   ALL SERVICES—AIR SEA RAIL INSURANCE ETC.

26th November 1948.

Mrs. J. Woodley,   Ref: RSH/ED
"The Cot",
St. Nicholas at Wade,
Nr. Birchington, Kent.

Dear Madam,

                        Travel to Australia.

          We have very much pleasure in confirming our
telephone conversation of this morning when we informed
you that three seats have been reserved for you and your
children to travel on the Constellation service BO.704/1
from London to Sydney, departing on the 1st December, and,
in this connection you will have to assemble at the Airways
Terminal, Buckingham Palace Road, Victoria, S.W.1. by no
later than 09.15 hours on the morning of departure.

          We have reserved a double room with three beds,
for you to stay at the Grosvenor Hotel, Buckingham Palace
Road, for the night of the 30th November; this hotel is
only two hundred yards away from the Airways Terminal.

          It is advised that a free baggage allowance of
66 lbs. each is permitted, so your total allowance will
be 198 lbs. Should you desire to insure this, or yourself,
kindly complete the enclosed proposal forms and return to
us with the premiums, when we shall be happy to issue the
policies.

          Finally, we are attaching hereto an itinerary of
your journey, together with our account. Please confirm
that you will call at our office on Tuesday to pick up your
passport and the flight tickets. The only health regulations
required are, smallpox vaccination and it is duly noted that
you are in possession of the necessary certificates, and we
have had your passport stamped with this information.

                                    Yours faithfully,
                                    J. W. KEARSLEY & CO. LTD.

SOUTH AFRICAN OFFICE — J. W. KEARSLEY (S.A.) (Pty) LTD., Unity House, 100 Fox Street, JOHANNESBURG.
EAST AFRICAN OFFICE — J. W. KEARSLEY (E.A.) LTD., Windsor Street, DAR-ES-SALAAM.

across the cornfields and marshes to the North Sea beyond. I must not dwell on the past, I told myself. There is only the future, with hope of a better life and streets flowing with milk and honey if I am to believe all that John had written. Only time would tell!

26th November 1948.
Itinerary for Mrs. Woodley & 2 children.

			Flight
1.12.48.	Report Airways Terminal,		
	Buckingham Palace Rd. S.W.S.	09:15 hrs.	BO.704/1
	Depart London Airport	11.00 hrs.	" "
	Arrive Rome	15:45 hrs.	" "
2/12/48.	Depart Rome	06.15 hrs.	" "
	Arrive Cairo	12.25 hrs.	" "
	Depart Cairo	16.00 hrs.	" "
3.12.48.	Arrive Karachi	03.55 hrs.	" "
3.12.48	Depart Karachi	21.15 hrs.	" "
4.12.48	Arrive Calcutta	02.30 hrs.	" "
	Depart Calcutta	04.00 hrs.	" "
	Arrive Singapore	13.20 hrs.	" "
5.12.48	Depart Singapore	08.00 hrs.	" "
	Arrive Darwin	18.15 hrs.	" "
	Depart Darwin	23.15 hrs.	" "
6.12.48.	Arrive Sydney	08.00 hrs.	" "

Order of Equatorial Air Voyagers

Member

Know All Men By These Presents

that   MRS. J. M. WOODLEY

of

having this day flown over the Equator and having been
cleansed by flying through the Heavens of all offences and
malice, and the evils associated with Demons, Gremlins,
Poltergeists and other Devils of the middle air, has become
acceptable as a liege and loyal MEMBER of Our Royal
Demesne (Aerial Division).

Hereby,

all the Rights, Privileges and Benefits reserved for those
who take to the sky in airliners, are graciously bestowed.

The Royal Seal
hereon affixed

Neptune
Omnium Rex (Caelum)

Time: ol 3.2
Date: 5/12/48   Witness
Aircraft: R.M.A. G-ALAL   Commander
               "BANBURY"

Part Two

Australia 1948–1977

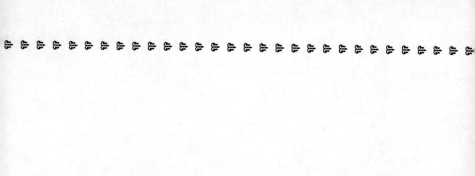

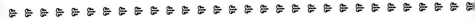

WALTZING MATILDA

Once a jolly swagman
Camped by a billabong,
Under the shade of a coolibah tree;
And he sang as he watched
And waited 'till his billy boiled,
"Who'll come a'waltzing Matilda with me."

—*A.B. "Banjo" Paterson*

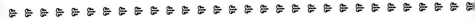

AUSTRALIA, THE PROMISED LAND

❧

$\mathcal{I}$ think my immediate impression was that I felt diminutive. The vastness of the continent, the huge sprawling cities and nothing but desert in between. After village life and the softness of the English countryside, I wondered how I would ever be able to adjust. And it was hot. The sun poured down from a merciless blue sky day after day. I felt trapped. Everything, and everyone I had known, was now half a world away.

John's early impressions and mine were very different. John had been in Australia six months before we arrived and had found accomodation in a friend's house. He had succeeded in leasing rooms in Melbourne's Collins Street and was establishing himself in a medical practice.

I had mixed feelings. Food was plentiful and the shops were filled with everything from clothes, to china imported from Britain. At first I thought how wonderful it all was then I felt anger. Here was everything that you could possibly wish for and poor old Britain had so little.

My early days were beset with problems. Ray developed measles before we even reached Sydney. We were still in the air when I noticed her eyes and the developing rash. Soon after our arrival Graham succumbed. It was December.

Christmas came and went and we were quarantined, unable to mix with the family with whom John had become friendly. It was blazingly hot and the spirit of celebration and all we were accustomed to gave way to beach parties.

Then I developed a rash. The doctor said it was a "good dose of poison ivy". The heat and irritation kept me awake at night. But the rash did not respond to treatment and I was sent to a specialist who pronounced an allergic reaction to something, possibly fruit. After numerous tests that proved negative the cause was found in the sun's rays. The resulting problems seemed insurmountable. It was impossible to buy clothes for women with long sleeves so I bought men's shirts and wore long skirts and always carried a sunshade.

For a while we rented a house in Malvern, one of Melbourne's suburbs. It was owned by an artist and she had a passion for flamingos. There were pink flamingos even in the bedroom, they peered at us from every room. John loathed them and removed the painting from above our bed and hid it underneath. Mrs. Gerrenko was mad with annoyance and threatened to evict us. So when John was out, and to pacify her, I rehung the bird and dared John to remove it a second time!

In the meantime we spent our weekends looking for somewhere to live and found an almost completed new house on the outskirts of Melbourne. It was not long before it was finished and the builders and painters had all left. It was an exciting new project, our own first home. We bought furniture made from the local silky oak, a beautiful blond wood, and moved in.

The summer had been hot but now it was June, the

Australian winter. It was cold and wet with a penetrating rawness. In the livingroom was a fireplace. We bought logs and sometimes we drove into the hills nearby and gathered wood. The evenings were always cosy and it reminded us of home and England.

But our woes were not over. Ray started school nearby, and before the end of the first term there was an outbreak of poliomylitis. My sense of humour completely deserted me: I felt utter desolation. Never again would I see my father. Ray, too, missed her grandfather and could not understand why he did not come and live with us.

There was much anguish in those early days and I wondered how we could have left England and all that was dear to us. After almost a year and much discussion John and I decided to go to Brisbane, in Queensland, to see what our prospects were there. We left Ray and Graham in Happy Hollow, a nursery school in the hills nearby. I was saddened leaving them, watching their little faces as we drove away filled me with sorrow and doubt... were we doing the right thing?

John was given introductions to some of the doctors there and on one occasion he was invited to a luncheon at the United Services Club. To John's surprise, sitting opposite him was a man he knew – Stephen Suggit, an ear, nose and throat specialist. John, Stephen and his wife, Winifred, knew each other in London before the war. John was excited when he returned to me later that evening. Stephen and Gwen welcomed us and invited us to dinner. They were enthusiastic about their life in the new country. "You will love it here, everything is different, the vegetation, tropical fruits, the people and the way of life. You must come!"

Their enthusiasm was infectious. John and I returned to our hotel and before going to sleep we agreed to see a Real Estate Agent. Sleep eluded me. Instinctively I knew our lives were about to change.

The next morning the sun was shining and we set out with an air of optimism. We found a Realtor who drove us to Ascot, a suburb of Brisbane and the first house he showed us was perfect. There were bananas growing in the garden, citrus fruits of all kinds, monsterias that ran wild and produced elongated fruits that tasted similar to fruit salad. It was such a contrast to the place we were planning to leave that for the first time since leaving England, I felt happy.

We bought the house. Now we had two homes. In order to buy the Brisbane building we had to sell the one in Melbourne. We flew home to a wonderful reunion with Ray and Graham. We immediately put the house on the market. Our good fortune was holding – the agent knew a retired couple, country people who wanted to move to Melbourne. The agent brought them over, they liked it and wanted to buy but they wanted it fully furnished. How could they? Our beautiful furniture! The dispute went on and on but they remained adamant so we had no alternative but to agree to the buyers' demands.

Life became hectic with last minute preparations. I put the children to bed. It was our last night in Melbourne. I slept little. The dark night changed slowly to a grey pallid dawn before I woke them. While they slept I prepared the breakfast and cut sandwiches for the journey. Our personal belongings had been packed into teachests and dispatched by carrier, John had bought a small trailer, a Tom Thumb. In it he put our

remaining belongings and the last minute items. We were
ready and waiting and still the new owners and the agent had
not arrived. My worst fear now was that they would back out
of the agreement. They eventually arrived one hour late and
with a sigh of relief we waved good-bye and set off.

A thousand miles lay ahead of us. We camped along
the way. The children slept in the car and John and I slept in a
small tent. The ground was warm and dry. All thought of
snakes that I most feared faded from my consciousness as the
crickets sang well into the night and the eucalyptus trees gave
us shelter. Everyone was happy!

We bought vegetables and to pass the time the children
and I prepared them for the evening meal which we cooked
over an open fire. We sang nursery rhymes and rounds end-
lessly. Crossing the mountain passes the noise of the cicadas
was deafening and the further north we drove the hotter it
became and the louder the cicadas sang.

We had been on the road for two days and were crossing a mountain range when there was a terrible scraping
sound. We looked through the rear window of the car and
watched as Tom Thumb slid backwards, gathering momen-
tum as it slipped away and finally crashed into the
mountainside on the bend of the road. Briefly we were all
speechless. John let the car roll slowly backwards towards the
trailer that had disintegrated spilling the contents over the
road. We gathered blankets, sheets, pots and pans and stowed
everything into the car for the children to arrange themselves
on and squeezed the overflow into the boot. We were inexpe-
rienced and had no idea the road conditions could be so harsh.
I forget what happened to Tom Thumb, he has been obscured

by time.

We had planned to take five days over the journey but as we were preparing the evening meal on our third day, John exclaimed in a burst of excitement, "We must hurry, we have to arrive tomorrow!"

"Why the change of plan when we are all enjoying our new found freedom?" I asked.

"Here, read this!" John handed me the *Australian Medical Journal*. Ralph Thatcher, John's boyhood friend was doing a locum in Brisbane.

"We must get there before they move on."

John and Ralph had been to school together in London but during the war they had lost touch with one another. Now on the other side of the world chance would reunite them if we could arrive in time.

The kookaburra's raucous laughter woke us early and while the children splashed in the creek like little nymphs, I prepared breakfast before setting off on our last leg of the journey.

As we passed through Brisbane we had an appointment with the solicitor. The finalization of our new home had yet to be ratified. The journey had been arduous and dusty. Even though we kept the windows securely closed the dust found its way into everything. I had packed a change of clothes for John and the children but I had forgotten a change for myself. This delayed us. We had to find a store. The sales lady, a kindly soul, let me tidy myself in the washroom and I exchanged my grubby shorts and shirt for a pretty pink and grey dress, suitably clad to meet the solicitor.

With the formalities behind us we found our way to

Ascot. Our road was lined with palm trees and how beautiful and tropical they looked. There was a short drive: To the right a few steps led to the balcony and a door opened into the main room. There was a large bay-window with cushioned seat, wood panelled walls, double-doors led into the diningroom and the kitchen beyond. On our left were the bedrooms and another balcony where the children slept.

We had arrived in Melbourne exactly one year ago. Now one year later, almost to the day, we reached Brisbane. Although we had no furniture we slept on the floor, sat on tea-chests and enjoyed our brief camping spree in our own home. John made contact with the Thatchers who were as excited as we were. We invited them to join us Christmas Day.

Ralph and Mary were new arrivals like ourselves. They also had two children of similar ages, Sarah and Roger. Moving one's roots from one country to another is not easy. Missing family and friends is made easier when the experiences are shared and as the days passed our friendships grew and our longing for England lessened. And this our second Christmas we shared and toasted each other with champagne and to the future that seemed more promising than at any time since our arrival in Australia.

Queensland offered a more leisurely way of life. The Queenslanders were gentle, softly spoken people. Doors and windows were left open shielded by wire screens and outside awnings covered the verandahs.

We ate tropical fruits fresh from the garden, bananas, huge bunches hung from the trees that grew to be fifteen to twenty feet high, citrus fruits: oranges, grapefruit, cumquats that made marmalade and delicious brandy, lemons, papaws and monsterias. The tropical flowers were more colourful than any of us could have imagined – red flame trees, blue jacarandas, hibiscus and bougainvilleas flourished in the hot dry summer. And at night, the sweet scent of the lemon blossoms and frangipani lingered on the night air.

So we entered into a new period of time – new home, new schools, new friends, an era of hope. It was as John had written to me before we left England, a country of great promise.

ASCOT AND BEYOND

☙

*T*he Ascot home was perfect for the four of us. Every afternoon about three o'clock a cool breeze came. We could hear it before it arrived – a swishing sound in the palms, quite unlike the sound of the wind in any other trees, and we left the doors and windows wide open to embrace it. Ray started school a short walking distance away. I bought a bicycle with a carrier on the back for Graham and took him to pre-school each day. And we bought a puppy Tess, a bull terrier. Mary and I became close friends. Every weekend Ralph and Mary, John and I and the four children continued to explore different areas where there were creeks and water for the children to splash and play in and if they were lucky they would see turtles swimming in and out of the grasses in search of food. Sometimes we explored rain forests with leeches that wound themselves round the children's toes. We discovered new and exotic plants, bright and vividly coloured butterflies. Life was good, every day a new experience.

I specialized in making terrariums. I bought large brandy balloons and had glass lids made to seal in the moisture. The rain forests were the perfect places to gather mosses, inverted into brandy glasses and filled with soil from the creek and with the aid of tweezers I planted tiny tree seedlings.

Placed under table lamps overnight appeared colourful fungi in amongst the trees. It was a fascinating hobby.

The garden was a huge source of pleasure and supply. In addition to all the tropical fruits, small tomatoes reseeded themselves. There were brilliant red bottle-brush bushes in the front garden and I had my first encounter with a lizard. I thought it was a rock but could not recall seeing it there before and when I was about to pick it up it moved and out popped his head, legs and long tail. I thought he was magnificent and brought him a dish of bread and milk which he enjoyed. He was quite harmless and made a good and interesting pet – Lizzie, we named him.

Other pleasures were frogs, tree frogs, bright emerald green with long slender legs that sometimes hopped into the house looking for insects and we allowed them to stay as some of the indoor pests were far from welcome – cockroaches of all shapes and sizes from small ones that lived near water in the bathrooms and kitchens, to large ones that flew in from the palms. After living with it for a few months we discussed it with our neighbours who laughed it off, saying, "You'll get used to it"! Some things one can accept but not cockroaches! Every September during our years in Queensland we had the house fumigated. A team of men in masks sprayed, they called it 'fogging'. It left behind a white film on all the walls, floors, in cupboards and drawers. It not only dispersed cockroaches, but mosquitoes, flies, ants and spiders.

Australians were friendly sociable people and Brisbane was the perfect place for entertaining. As newcomers we were invited to numerous parties: dinner parties, cocktail parties, Sunday morning parties beneath the trees in the gardens and new friends were made. It was at a New Year's Eve party that we met an Englishman and his Danish wife, Mark and Lillie. He was an architect. We also met Mrs. Crocker who became our baby-sitter and an integral part of the family.

Eighteen months later with the advent of another baby we started searching for a larger home. We explored Hamilton Heights and found a timber dwelling with an iron roof surrounded by wide verandahs on all sides and built on fifteen foot high 'stumps' elevated to keep the house cool. We invited Mark to survey the building. It was the perfect family home with three bedrooms, each room opening on to the west verandah. Mark suggested plans for the nursery and June 2 1951 Jennefer was born.

The main room overlooked the Brisbane River with a limitless view of the cruise ships and float planes constantly on the move. Palm trees lined the water's edge, a city of twinkling lights in the evenings and twilight came early as we neared the equator and the sun dipped behind the nearby mountains. Mark proposed removing a large portion of the wall and replacing it with glass thus displaying the whole panoramic vista, an ever-changing picture and as Queensland homes were mostly built of timber at that time alterations were both quick and uncomplicated. We agreed with all his suggestions and the final result was a transformation, "what a view" everyone gasped when they walked into the room!

But there were certain disadvantages to living on top of a steep hill. Home-help was difficult to find and those who did come rarely returned. It was a busy time for me but it was a washerwoman's paradise! Nappies and sheets were put through the washing machine and hung on the rotary line.

The sun cast fine shadows from above and in a very short time everything was dry.

The months slipped by easily and peacefully and Christmas was fast approaching. I had everything prepared. The cake was made but not decorated when I went into hospital to have my fourth baby. My little Nicholas was born December 15 1952. Christmas Eve our neighbours called. I wished they would soon leave but as they showed no sign of doing so I withdrew to the kitchen as I still had not decorated the cake. I prepared the ingredients and inadvertently spilt the salt over the table and on to the floor. It was a bad omen and I should have found the time to clean it up. Instead, I slipped! My head caught the edge of the table. John rushed in to see what had happened and found me in a heap on the floor. He helped me to a chair and with my head resting on a bed of towels on the table, and after sterilizing a darning needle in boiling water he stitched the top of my ear into place. Christmas morning the bandages were removed and my hair carefully arranged to hide the ravages of the night before.

Our neighbours joined us. The smorgasbord feast was served outside on the verandah. There were fruits of all kinds fresh from the garden, cold turkey and green salads, papaws served with ice cream instead of plum pudding, citrus fruit cocktails, and bowls of sweet smelling passion flower blossoms for decoration. The cake never was decorated but no one seemed to notice.

☙ ☙ ☙ ☙ ☙ ☙

After six years, the heat and humidity began to take its

toll. January and February, the monsoon months were particularly trying as the humidity rose and the rains came. The house remained stiflingly hot. The cool breeze that came every afternoon in Ascot ceased as we were now on the other side of the hill. There were ripples of discontent among the English and one-by-one families began to drift south, and when the Thatchers left for Adelaide, we began to think about moving too.

Tasmania was a possibility. It was decided that I should go first and explore. I sailed across Bass Strait to Devonport in the north of the island and flew the remainder of the way to Hobart, the capital of Tasmania. It was the English who introduced the apple orchards many years ago and it became a thriving industry with exports all over the world.

Mount Wellington dominated the city and in the winter months it was covered in snow with good skiing. It also provided excellent walking with views across the strait to the nearby islands.

I talked with the local people, many of them were immigrants from England, all seemed to think it was the perfect place for happy family living. I explored the city with interest – there were schools and churches of all denominations, a university, parks and gardens, legislative buildings and hospitals.

There was much excitement when I arrived home. John wrote letters to the Royal Hobart Hospital and was assured of a position. Before leaving Brisbane we went to Lone Pine Koala Sanctuary. Hedges of lantanas, oleanders and bougainvilleas crowded in upon us as we crossed the wooden walkway over the creek and we were greeted by a large brown dog with a young koala sitting on its back, there were wombats, kanga-roos, emus, native birds and many other animals. The children were all allowed to hold a koala and that delighted them. It was our farewell outing together.

John flew to Hobart. He was the first to go. We all followed by sea.

It was not difficult to sell the house. I recall the day the agent brought a lady to inspect it. She flounced through, saw the view and with a quick peep at all the other rooms said to the agent, "That's it!" The agent turned to me and behind her back he gave me the thumbs-up sign.

John met us in Devonport in the north of the Island and we drove the rest of the way, a distance of about 150 miles. It was June, winter, and the trees were bare. The younger children couldn't understand why all the trees looked dead! Queensland had few deciduous trees unlike Tasmania that enjoyed the four changing seasons, so Tasmania, known as the Apple Isle, opened up a whole new way of life.

John had found us a house in Sandy Bay on the out-skirts of Hobart. It was a large home with garden overlooking the River Derwent. There was a gardener and fresh vegetables daily. Ray and Graham settled down in their new schools and we were established, or so we thought. We stayed one year. John was offered a senior position at the Launceston Hospital. It included all moving expenses, a hospital house rent free for one year. Our furniture was in storage as the house we were renting was fully furnished and only a minimum of packing was necessary. I had mixed feelings about leaving Hobart, but it was another experience.

There was much excitement as we all piled into the car

and drove north in search of our next adventure. The scenery was mainly farmlands and orchards, mountains and hills. On the way we visited the Birdlife and Animal Park as we had not seen any Tasmanian Devils and we were curious to see what they looked like. Tasmania has a wealth of animals in the wild, only to be found on the island, including five different kinds of reptiles, all of which are venomous so you had to watch where you were walking at all times. But the Devils, so aptly named, are fearsome looking beasts but despite their vicious appearance they do not harm humans, they are nocturnal and attack the farmers' sheep and poultry at night, which is why we had not seen them on our rambles.

With the aid of a map we found Hill Street. Being a hospital house I was not sure what to expect, and we were agreeably surprised when we arrived to find an attractive home with a cared-for garden. Because of the steep slope the house was built on two levels, both joined together by a glass covered stairway. The lounge was comfortable with a huge brick fireplace, and double doors led on to a patio and into the garden.

The garden had been landscaped in such a way that bushes flowered throughout the year. There was a large walnut tree in the front, and the back garden was a place to wander with two ponds and water-lilies growing, several different kinds of apples, grape vines, and flowering bushes. And there were possums nesting in the trees.

The climate was milder and drier than Hobart when many an afternoon the clouds drifted down from Mount Wellington, and it became dark an cold. The view overlooked the city of Launceston in the valley below, and on a misty autumn morning there were just the church spires floating on a cloud – the type of picture that would have inspired Hans Christian Andersen to write some of his fairy tales.

On our arrival we were greeted by a black cat and her three kittens. Alas, they were all diseased and with cries of protest from the children they had to be put to sleep but we compensated by giving Ray a puppy, Terry Oats, and Graham chose a kitten, Tigger. New schools were found for Ray and Graham and nearby was a pre-school for Jenny.

With spring just around the corner we began our search for a place to live. Instead of buying we thought it would be fun to build. At weekends we drove into the country near Launceston and explored. We found some parkland overlooking a forest and I said, "wouldn't it be wonderful if we could buy something like this?" The children clamoured excitedly around.

Not far away was a corner store. It was hot and the children thirsty and while we were buying this and that, John casually asked if there was any land for sale in the vicinity. The owner of the store, Mr. Dunstan, said, "I have some that might interest you." He locked up the premises and we walked through the village until we came to the very land we had just been thinking was an impossible dream. The land had to be surveyed – there were no roads, water or electricity. Flowering wattles and native gum trees flourished... it could not have been more idyllic.

We bought an acre and became land owners. We inherited possums, a marsupial animal that nested in the trees, and bandicoots that lived in burrows and ate insects; they too, were marsupials with pointed ears and sharp little faces. And, colourful birds, some of them unique to Tasmania.

We watched as the road developed and we found an architect. He drew up plans which were unsuitable and we wished Mark lived nearer, he would have understood our needs. So we worked independently with the builder, a Dutchman. Within a year we moved in. Our home faced north with large windows that captured the view of the forest and the sun streamed in during the winter months. Wide steps led to the entrance door and into the hall which was divided from the lounge by glass sliding doors and a picture view of the wide oval lawn sloping downwards and surrounded by trees. We cleared the undergrowth and some of the trees keeping only the wattles and each spring they were smothered in clusters of golden flowers.

In the diningroom we installed a pot-bellied stove. The kitchen was styled after the English pub with a large opening into the diningroom and pewter pots hung from above.

I could look through the kitchen window into the tree-tops and watch the birds. The wattle birds fascinated me as they hung upside-down and sucked the nectar from the flowers of the gums. We landscaped the garden and planted Japanese flowering cherries along the drive, and roses flourished in the clay soil. Those were happy days.

Launceston on the River Tamar was a small city with old-world buildings set amongst parks and gardens and it was one of the richest farming areas in Tasmania – it exported wool, apples and vegetables, minerals and timber.

There was the usual round of parties and school functions and Nick commenced school. The park we overlooked was named the Punch Bowl. It sloped down into a hollow that ran beside a golf course and on the far side was Nick's school. Each day, before and after school, I walked with him until he became accustomed to walking through the park alone.

Now I must digress briefly: When my sister, Molly, was demobilized after the war she went to South Africa – it had always been her ambition. It was there that she met her husband, John McAndrew. They had two sons, Shaun and Peter. While we were enjoying our rural life in Tasmania a letter from Molly arrived with the news that John McAndrew had applied for a transfer to Melbourne. This was wonderful news as our children had grown up without knowing their cousins. When they arrived we flew to Melbourne to welcome them and there was a happy reunion as we had not seen each other for many years. What a lot we had to talk about! While we were enjoying our final drink together Molly commented on the number of moves we had made. I remember saying, "I think I could live anywhere now!" Without a word John pulled a bit of newsprint from his pocket and showed me an advertisement: It was for a Director of Anaesthesiology at one of Melbourne's hospitals. He said he was thinking of applying. My world was shattered. I knew our days in Tasmania were coming to an end.

John left Launceston soon afterwards and I was left to bring up the rear. I was experienced in selling homes but this time I was less enthusiastic. So the house that we had worked so hard to perfect was sold and taking all our possessions including the cat and the dog we returned to Melbourne, all except Ray who had just left school and had been accepted at the Launceston General Hospital in the haematology department.

We found a house in Balwyn a suburb of Melbourne. The house was old by Australian standards, solid and with a look of permanency. An attractive pillared porch led into the hall. It was a well planned home with lounge, diningroom, study. Graham, Jenny and Nick all started at new schools.

Soon after we moved in I was sitting in the kitchen surrounded by boxes when there was a tap at the door and a voice called out, "May I come in?"

"Please do," I said.

In her hands she carried a tray with teapot and freshly baked scones. "I thought you might like a cup of tea, I'm Gwenda, I live next door."

Dear Gwenda! Never was a cup of tea more welcome. While she helped unpack some of the boxes she told me she was a widow with four children. I liked her. We became instant friends.

The house we had bought somewhat hurriedly was far too costly and we decided to use it as a stepping-stone. Gwenda told me about Blackburn, an outer suburb, known as the bell-bird area. She drove me there one morning and as we got out of the car we were greeted by a chorus of bells. we just stood and listened, it was remarkably beautiful. I was instantly endeared to the place. Later, I told John about it and the following day we returned and explored the area more closely. He was intrigued by the birds but more especially by a large old modernized farmhouse that had a 'For Sale' sign outside. It was empty and we peeped through the windows. Our excitement grew. We couldn't wait to get home to call the agent. An appointment was made. It was a lovely family home, just right for all of us. It was a long way from the city but there was a

good train service. We decided to buy. 'Crazy' some people
called us. But to us, it was fun!

No change of schools was necessary and we had a few
very happy years there. The bellbirds were a constant fascination as they fluttered about in the eucalyptus trees – they were
small, moss-green and regarded it as their territory keeping
all the other wild birds away. We were now living in a forest
of eucalypts and lilly pilly trees, not conducive to growing
flowers or vegetables but we had a collection of animals and
birds, tortoises and turtles, guinea-pigs and hamsters, an avi-
ary with budgerigars, Brutus, a colourful pink and grey galah
(a member of the parrot family), and how he talked – he
mimicked everything we said. Our neighbour had a smoker's
cough, he copied that and when we laughed he joined in the
chorus!

One afternoon Nick arrived home from school.

"Look what I've got!" he said, as he pulled a newly
hatched duckling out of his pocket. He said it was part of a
science project. I wondered what to feed it. Nick suggested
bread and milk and he loved it. He tossed his little head around
and the food splashed all over the kitchen floor. The children
named him Critchlow. At bedtime we made up a bed in a box
of towels with a small desk lamp for warmth and covered it
all with another towel. That was his "possie."

I became Critchlow's surrogate mother. He followed
me everywhere. One day I could have wept – I trod on his
wee foot, and how he cried: I never would have believed that
anything so small could make so much noise! After that I
bought a pair of furry yellow slippers and Critchlow snuggled
into them like a nest.

But the years passed all too quickly. The children grew up and became young adults. Ray completed her nursing training and emigrated to Canada. Jenny commenced her nursing training in Melbourne. And Graham was called up. In the mid-1960s, fighting in Vietnam intensified, the United States increased its military aid by sending servicemen to South Vietnam. Why the Australian young men of nineteen were called up to support the Americans in Vietnam, I do not know or understand, and never will.

I wandered through the children's empty rooms and wished I could turn back the clock. Our beautiful home with all its fond memories, was now too large.

After much thought and discussion we decided to return to Balwyn. We found a house with an exquisite blue jacaranda tree beside the entrance door. There were lemons and figs growing in the garden that led into a park and the garden was smaller and more manageable with songful magpies in the eucalyptus trees.

Magpies are easily tamed. We bought minced meat and each day they came. They landed on the patio and warbled, a gentle continuous trilling sound, they became so tame they would even wander into the house. De Grood was wonderful: he used to sit on the patio and watch with his front paws crossed but never disturbed the birds.

De Grood was our black Labrador dog – he was my constant companion. He probably saved my life on one occasion. I had taken him for his run before settling in for the night and as we neared home he moved close beside me. A low growl rumbled gently within him and the hair on his coat bristled. Our street was lined with lilly pilly trees. Their thick glossy foliage cast dark shadows across the pavement. Groody continued to stay close to me and as we neared home he moved slowly ahead until, in the shadows of the trees, was a tall, heavily-built man. Groody went to him, bared his teeth and growled – not a gentle rumble, but a loud, threatening warning. I walked past the man while Groody kept guard. He wouldn't let him move and remained crouched ready to pounce, until I reached home.

At the gate I turned to him and called. Groody gave a loud warning bark, before bounding to me. He was a dear dog, we all loved him and it was a sad day for everyone when he was hit by a car and killed. Nick buried him in the garden and planted some daffodils. Now, each year in the springtime, there is a carpet of gold to immortalize him.

ENGLAND REVISITED

&

I looked through the window of the Boeing 707 and watched the sunrise, the pale glow of the early morning sky, the harsh desert below shimmering in haze, and I knew Sydney was in for another scorching hot day. Twenty six years had passed since leaving England and I was on my way to visit family and friends.

I flew to Heathrow, via Bahrain and Singapore. On arrival I hailed a taxi and went straight to the Royal Overseas League, my Headquarters, and fell asleep. When I awoke, having slept through breakfast, I lifted the blind and looked through the window and viewed Green Park shining in the morning sunlight and the early spring foliage.

Hastily, I dressed and wandered in the park. I followed the smartly dressed men and women who were all walking purposefully in one direction and I found myself entering the Chapel Royal and being shown a seat. I received Holy Communion with the Queen's Chaplain: an unexpected awesome experience. I continued my walk through Green Park to Buckingham Palace and photographed the Queen's residence. By this time I was hungry. Bread and wine is no substitute for breakfast and I hurried back to the club.

It was good to see family and friends again, nothing

had changed, we were all a bit older and wiser but it was as though I had never been away as we talked about old times. Before going to Australia I had seen little of England because of the war but during my stay I wanted to see as much as possible. Eric, my brother suggested Lands End would be a good place to commence my journey.

After Australia, England was cool but I had a warm woollie and I could always buy more if needed. I liked Lands End and walked many miles over the cliffs: the air was fresh and invigorating, and I thought of the days of smuggling and how easy it must have been to get their contraband into the country with a coastline wide open.

Penzance, the most westerly town in England had a warm climate and a profusion of flowers even in the winter-time. A pleasant little town but too popular for my liking, the cafes and streets crowded with holiday-makers.

I sailed in the steam ship *Scillonian* to the Scilly Isles and wandered through Tresco's Abbey Gardens with its collection of tropical flowers and plants. The clouds began to gather. Rain set in on the return trip and I was drenched. I had found a bed-and-breakfast for the night and a kind stranger visiting from Oxford, lent me a robe and we drank hot cocoa while my clothes dried before the fire.

I toured Yorkshire and the Bronte country. It brought to life, and into focus, all I had read about the family. The moors, desolate and grey the day I was there, fascinated me. I was drawn to walk on them, I met no one, not a soul, just sheep with long tails and shaggy coats.

From there I moved on to St. Andrew's. (I travelled everywhere by bus, it was both economical and comfortable.)

For many people St. Andrew's spells nothing more than golf but there is much much more to it than that. It is an historic city with a cathedral dating back to the twelfth century. The St. Andrew's university is the oldest university in Scotland. Before leaving there I climbed to the top of St. Rule's Tower and spread before me was a splendid view of the city and panorama of land and sea.

Scotland is a rugged, mountainous country. Dark clouds often blanket the land and storms sweep in from the Atlantic. Edinburgh, the capital is steeped in history. The castle stands on a rocky hill and dominates the city. The Palace of Holyrood House was built in the 1500s. Mary, Queen of Scots, married her second husband there. Today it is the official residence of the Queen during her visits to Scotland.

Ray and I met in Edinburgh. We hired a Renault 5 and went island hopping. After viewing the highlights of Edinburgh we drove to Largs, and stayed at the Curlinghall Hotel, overlooking the Firth of Clyde. It rained most of the day but it did not concern us, the hotel was warm, the food good, and there was a huge log-fire burning. We read, rested, and had much to talk about: we had not seen each other for years.

The next day we left Largs by ferry for the Isle of Arran. We stayed at the Kildonan Hotel, owned by Charles Ash, the artist. The hotel stood almost on the water's edge and we scrambled over the rocks, seabirds our only companions. Charles Ash had captured it all on canvas – it was beautiful in a rugged sort of way.

We visited Oban, and Iona and the Isle of Mull where St. Columba from Ireland first preached in the sixth century.

Columba's Monastery has long since gone but the remains of
a later one have been renovated and rebuilt. Iona is now regarded as one of the holy places of the world. The Abbey
quite beautiful with a large Celtic cross standing outside as
though to invite us in. Sheep roam the rocky outcrops and
few people live there.

We crossed the Sound of Sleat to reach the Isle of Skye.
"Over the Sea to Skye"; We learnt the song so long ago when I
was at school and the tune went round and round in my head.
Some people called it the Misty Isle. We were told that the
Island had many scenic wonders to offer. I recorded in my
diary, "It began to rain, first lightly and then with spite. There
is something about Skye and the Sound of Sleat that attracts
the most baleful clouds in the North Atlantic. It poured!"
Found a bed-and-breakfast for the night.

Left Bradford, on the Isle of Skye early and drove to
Uig. We crossed the Minch to the Outer Hebrides and
Stornoway on the Isle of Lewis. Stornoway has a busy harbour
and is the centre of the Harris Tweed industry. I bought
woollen underwear. We explored the island, driving and walking. It was here that we discovered the village of Callanish
and the remarkable standing stones said to be over 2000 years
old. It was a good day. We scrambled over the hills and saw
black houses, thatched roofed cottages and sheep on the roof-
tops. The beaches were pure white.

We returned to the mainland and the weather improved.
We followed the Caledonian Canal, along Glen More and Loch
Ness to Inverness. Apart from a dominating Castle on top of a
hill Inverness had little to offer. We drove on to Thurso, the
port for the Orkney and Shetland Islands, a busy small town

and salmon fishing in season. We flew to Kirkwall on the Orkney Island. We wanted to go by ferry but the weather wild and the water turbulent we had no alternative but to fly. Kirkwall, a fascinating place, full of interest from St. Magnus Cathedral founded in 1157, a magnificent memorial to Saint Magnus; the Bishop's Palace with its round tower to the quaint streets, and good and varied shops.

The Orkneys consist of about a hundred islands many of them rich in historic remains of life in the Orkneys from prehistory to the present century. We enjoyed the sense of space and freedom from restrictions imposed by modern city life; the birds, the wild life and the remarkable coast scenery where time did not seem to matter, where the simple delights still had value.

We returned to Thurso and on to John O'Groats and stayed at the John O'Groats Hotel, an unusual building, built on the headland and octagonal in design. The further north we drove the wilder the coastline became, rugged shorelines, massive cliffs, fewer and fewer people, isolated crofts and plenty of sheep, seals cavorting through the waves, others sprawled out over the rocks, and hundreds of birds all jostling for a position on the cliff ledges.

We drove to Duncansby and climbed the many spiral iron steps to the top of the lighthouse and looked through the telescope across the Pentland Firth in the direction of Scapa Flow, an important naval base throughout the two world wars. During World War II a German submarine torpedoed the British battleship *Royal Oak*. Over eight hundred officers and men lost their lives that night.

We spent one night in Stirling and stayed at the Golden

Lion, a charming place, lovely hotel, interesting castle that dates back to the fifteenth and sixteenth centuries. The castle stands on top of a precipitous rock and was the favourite home of several Scottish kings.

Then on to the mountainous Cairngorms. We rode the chair-lift to within 500 feet of the summit. And my, how cold it was! I was glad of my woollen vest and bloomers, but it was not enough to keep out the bitter wind and snow. Time was running out. We left the Cairngorms for Edinburgh. We booked into the North British Hotel and returned the Renault. We would be leaving for London the next day.

We booked into the Charing Cross Hotel. In the evening we went to see Sid James in *Carry on London*, a riotously funny play. The next day, our last, we dined a'Top The Revolving Tower. It was a glorious evening. The sun shone and London looked its best.

I went with Ray to Heathrow. It had been a holiday to remember. Farewells are never pleasant but we had our diaries and photographs to tell the tale. We hugged each other and waved good-bye.

I had seen more of the British Isles than ever before – from Lands End in the south, to John O'Groats in the north, a distance of 876 miles, the two furthest points on the map.

I returned to the League. I still had time before returning home. Perhaps I could get a job, I thought. But, doing what? I discussed it with my uncle – he thought the whole idea ridiculous.

"Come and live here," he said.

However, I pursued the notion without his blessing and it was not long before I returned to him triumphant.

I had scanned the *London Times* and the *Daily Telegraph*.
There were heaps of jobs for nannies and housekeepers, and
an agency that promised to Solve Your Problem.

BROADLAND PARK

꩜

$\mathcal{J}$aking the underground to Kensington I found the agency and with much aplomb walked in. A friendly woman greeted me and asked if she could help.

"Yes," I said, "I need a short term job." She picked five cards from her file. I had a choice. I chose the one I thought I would be able to do.

The interview took place in Kensington Palace Gardens off Bayswater Road in London where many ambassadors to the Court of St. James have their residences. While we drank tea from fine bone china Lady Isabella told me about her uncle who needed someone to care for him while his companion/nurse was in hospital recovering from the shingles.

The following day we drove to Broadland Park in Sussex. It was a mansion! The uncle was a tall, handsome man in his late seventies. He lived alone with his dog in three hundred acres of woodlands, cornfields and green pastures. At the entrance was the Lodge.

On arrival it was as though I had stepped back in time. I was introduced to all the staff. Each member had his or her own role to play from those who cleaned the brass and copper, to the chauffeur, and the gardener who supplied the vegetables. When the day ended the staff returned to the village and there were just the two of us. Before leaving, the odd-job man offered to lock-up and close the windows. I asked him to show me the routine as it was June and the evenings were long – it seemed a pity to close out the sunshine and the daylight hours. The windows and the shutters were immense and a heavy iron rod had to be swung across to secure them.

I was shown over the house from the kitchen to the butler's pantry and through the many rooms including the Honourable Simon Delaney's study, where he spent most of his time when he was not on the estate. The study was the most interesting room of them all. Simon had a collection of paintings adorning the walls, paintings of naval battles in the 18th century, and the famous Admiral Rodney, of whom Simon claimed to be a direct descendant. Another collectors' item was a blue velvet chair that had belonged to Queen Elizabeth at the time of her coronation. He was also Winston Churchill's cousin.

A blue carpet covered the wide staircase that led from the centre of the flagstone hall to a semi-circular balcony with suites leading from it. Mine was at the opposite end of the gallery to Simon Delaney's. I had a rose coloured carpet, some books, and a desk, fireplace, and a huge four-poster bed. The view from the windows looked across the estate in the front, over a sea of golden cornfields and green pastures with a few Friesian black and white cows dotted about. It was supremely peaceful. At the back my suite overlooked the cobbled courtyard and stables. Only one horse remained, a chestnut stallion that Simon named Simple.

Once the staff had left for the day everything seemed quiet and strange as it always does in unfamiliar places. I wandered to the kitchen, there was an Aga cooker. I remembered my mother cooking with one many years ago and how delicious were her rock buns and scones and hoped mine would be as good. The floor was of flagstone and there was a large deal table in the centre of the room. The brasses on the walls shone from years of polish, reflecting images, making the space around bright and light.

After dinner Simon Delaney showed me the estate. We took Peter, the dog, on our walk. There was a walled garden for vegetables and fruit trees of all kinds. The paths were lined with herbaceous beds. Roses and sweetpeas filled the night air with fragrance. Simon's pride was his greenhouse collection of orchids and other exotic plants which we watered together before wandering home when Simon decided to go to his room. I went with him, turned down his bed covers and left him with his book.

Taking Peter again, I walked all round the building as I wanted to know how many exits there were, and to make sure all the doors were locked and the windows secured. I followed the dog to a field that led to a creek. It was a glorious evening, the moon cast long shadows over the property making the world around us appear ethereal. I thought how fortunate I was to be living in such beautiful surroundings and being paid for the privilege of being there.

On our return I again peeped at Simon Delaney to make sure everything was well with him. The dog put himself to bed on the stairs under the chandelier that was left burning all night like a beacon.

After a while I, too, went to my room. Climbing into bed I had visions of the people who might have lived there, the type of life they would have lived, the balls, the gowns and the hunting parties. For some reason an unease began to creep over me, and a chill that was quite unreasonable and unexplainable. I tried to sleep and must have dozed because I woke with a start when there was a loud thump. I sat bolt upright and listened – had I dreamed it? And what of the man I was supposed to be looking after? I knew nothing of him. I heard sounds, and in my subconscious mind recalled the hollow ring of loose flagstones as I was being shown through the hall. Getting off my bed as quietly as possible I crept to the window. In the silence everything seemed to creak. I did not know what I expected to see and in the moonlight could see nothing, and no one. Then a door slammed! I shot with the speed of terror into Simon Delaney's room only to find him fast asleep.

I shook him saying, "There is someone in the house!"

He looked at me as though I may be a little touched and said, "You stay here."

But I wouldn't, and together we went down the staircase that passed the diningroom. The door, that I knew I had closed, was open.

"My God," he exclaimed, "we've been burgled!" The drawer from the sideboard was missing together with all the silver cutlery.

"Call the police," Simon shouted. I dashed to the butler's pantry and rang.

Without further thought I grabbed Peter and we ran round the house and through the gardens following footmarks imprinted in the dewey grass which led straight to the creek, and there we lost them. Thwarted, I returned home with

Peter bounding along beside me.

Simon was sitting in his study and beginning to show signs of shock. As I couldn't find his robe and he didn't know where it was, I wrapped him in a blanket and gave him a strong whisky. We waited in the study until the police arrived with tracker dogs. They scoured the grounds, but found nothing other than the footprints. They concluded that the thieves with their spoil had walked along the creek bed to a waiting car on the road, and they would already be on their way across the English Channel to France where it would all be sold. The police left promising to return when it was light.

I took Simon back to his room, but sleep eluded me. To pass the time I went down to the kitchen to make some tea and was shocked to find a man there – it was the Lodge gate-keeper.

"Did they take much?" he asked.

"How did you know?" I retorted.

He turned deathly white, then flushed and left abruptly. When he had gone I made sure the door was locked from the inside and the bolt securely drawn. But it unnerved me and I wished the night would end.

When the police returned Simon took them through the house to see what was missing. The study remained undisturbed. Across the hall, opposite the study, was the drawingroom completely ransacked and stripped of all its antiques and valuable silver pieces. Evidentally, they took the drawer from the diningroom, through the drawingroom, throwing into it everything they could quickly gather and left through the double doors at the far end of the room leading to the garden. Nothing was ever recovered.

The mystery remained. Who had done it? My belief was that someone knew the house and the area. The dog had not barked. Why? My mind went back to the man in the kitchen. Later, I learned he had been dismissed and although I do not believe he did it, I think he knew who did.

Their means of entry was at the rear of the house. A low oblong window ran parallel with the passage. The bar across the window was a long heavy wooden beam and with years of wear and tear it had worn away. With the aid of a crowbar they broke the window and moved the bar from side to side until it was loose enough to be lifted and thrown to the floor. That was the thump that initially woke me.

Following the stresses of my first night at Broadland Park life settled down to a more conventional symmetry. Simon and I became good friends. We walked many miles together, either on the estate or through the country lanes that bounded his property. Occasionally, the chauffeur drove us and we looked at old churches, and pubs where we stopped for a pint of the best draught beer and chatted with the locals. In the evenings we played cribbage and many a time Simon liked me to read to him. He relished the peace that came with night-fall and sitting round the log fire before retiring. Simon was a typical English gentleman with his smoking jacket, slippers and pipe, his long legs stretched out towards the fire, and Peter curled up beside him.

I enjoyed my six weeks at Broadland Park. It provided a unique and unforgettable experience. It also confounded my critics!

MY SYMBOL OF PEACE

❧

*T*he time came for me to leave London. We said good-bye and promised to write often. We flew to Frankfurt, Singapore, Sydney and Melbourne. A glorious morning welcomed me – spring blossoms everywhere.

It was good to be home and to sleep in my own bed again. But, it was not long before I realized nothing had changed. Our marriage, strained before I went away, remained the same. John went sailing every weekend. I looked after the home and garden and entertained my friends. Sometimes I went into the foot-hills of the nearby Dandenong Ranges where tree-ferns were plentiful and the lyrebirds sang, eucalyptus and wildflowers flourished. It was there that I found my little oasis, my symbol of peace.

THE MAGIC OF THE HILLS

&

$\mathcal{T}$he road wound its way round the mountain to the little village of Olinda. There you could buy knick-knacks, and postcards with views of the surrounding hills, wild animals that inhabited the forest, and native birds. From the bakery you could buy bread fresh from the oven, and enjoy Devonshire teas while sitting on the verandah under the colourful umbrellas watching the people passing and listening to the clip-clop of horses' hooves as they cantered by. There was a post office and general store, a garage, and a Real Estate Agent. Alfred Adams was his name.

One day I called to see him. "I am searching for a small cottage," I said.

He pulled out his file.

"I will drive you round now if you are free, and you can see what is available!"

He locked up and we got into the car. I enjoyed the sightseeing tour but all the trees were blackened by years of bushfires and I had lived in Australia long enough to know the hazards. Alfred understood my fears and promised to call me in a few days time.

When the call came I hopped into my little mini and rushed off. It was early morning when the eucalypts and tree-

ferns emanated a subtle fragrance. The air was fresh, everywhere peaceful with only the sounds of the birds mixed with
the chatter of parrots, contrasting vividly with the smog and
heat of Melbourne.

On arrival I hurried into the office and asked Alfred
what he had to show me.

"Come," he said, "hop in, you will like it."

We drove to the top of the Dandenong Ranges and followed a byroad that wound its way down a dirt road. It was
pretty with a grass verge and eucalyptus trees on either side.
As we neared the cottage Alfred told me about the owner and
described her as being 'a little eccentric.' She had designed
the cottage herself and would sell conditionally – she must
like the intended buyer.

It was a wonderful location. Hills and mountains surrounded the area, and as we walked down the winding drive
I saw between the trees, glimpses of a bright yellow door. I
noticed especially the trees, none of them was blackened: some-
how the mountains deflected the draft away from the home-
stead.

The cottage overlooked the valley known as the Patch,
a fertile area where market gardeners grew crops of vegetables
and berries and a creek ran through the property. After show-
ing me the cottage Nancy Cranston put the kettle on and we
sat and talked. I felt my adrenalin rising. I asked her why
there was no fireplace.

"I'm afraid of fires," Nancy explained, "especially as I
only use the cottage at weekends."

I bought the cottage complete with built-in furniture
without any second thoughts. Afterwards, I realized the

enormity of my undertaking. But even though I had to earn the money to make the payments I knew it was a good investment.

I found employment with a group of Accountants and advertised in the Melbourne Age for a tenant. The response was good and within two years the cottage and three acres of land was mine.

After completing the purchase, Jenny and I spent our first weekend there. Now that we were the proud possessors of the cottage we had time to examine and poke around. It was built of white painted timber with a bright yellow louvered door opening on to a flagstone porch. Another door led into the main room. The landscape offered an unobstructed view of the trees that sloped into the valley below and on a clear day, there was the ocean beyond. There was electricity and telephone, and a rain-water butt at the back, the water being heated by a small briquette heater. It was a fully self-contained little rural hideaway.

We wandered in the garden but it was hot and sultry and towards evening the sky grew dark and the air stilled ominously. A flock of black cockatoos screeched over like a cloud and settled in the trees silencing all the other birds of the forest.

We prepared dinner. The oven worked well and while we were enjoying our meal a wind sprang up gusting around the building.

We watched the storm crash through the forest and without warning we were plunged into darkness when a tree blew down across the road, smashing through power lines. I was glad we had heeded Nancy's warning, "always have a supply of candles handy," she said, "because you never know when you might need them." We went to bed but in the middle of the night the storm returned. We watched the lightning flicker and flash, trees lashed to a frenzy by the howling wind. When daylight came the rain had ceased, the air cleared and the black cockatoos had vanished.

Jenny and I donned our rubber boots and went outside to survey the damage. The air was crisp and cool after the oppressiveness of the night and everywhere emitted the pungent fragrance of eucalypts. Large branches had snapped and fallen over the trail leading to the creek. We detoured into the surrounding forest and as we wandered, gathering mushrooms as we went, we saw smoke rising through the trees.

"Look," said Jenny, "someone lives there. Let's go and see who it is."

As we neared the cottage we heard music. We stopped and listened. We peeped through the window and could see a young man playing the guitar. When he saw us he came outside and introduced himself.

"I'm Brett. I'm about to put the kettle on. Would you like a cup of coffee?"

We accepted his invitation. It was a nice snug little cottage and a fire was glowing in the fireplace. Using long handled wire forks we made toast. We talked about the hills and I wondered why this young man lived alone in so remote a place. As though he read my thoughts Brett told of his early life on a sheep property in Tasmania so we had much to talk about and many experiences to share.

"My passion is music," he said. "I love the hills, they offer peace at the end of the day when I can compose and meditate."

I liked this young man who lived alone, who sought the comfort of the hills, and God – and found both.

& & & & & & &

I was barely awake one morning listening to the forest sounds when I heard a dull thud against the fly screen door. I peeped out and there he was!

"Hello, Little One!" I said.

His dark brown eyes focused fearlessly on me. Gently I opened the door while speaking quietly to him. He sniffed my shoes and ankles and he allowed me to touch his soft warm body covered in brown fur from the tip of his tail, to the tips of his ears and whiskers. Little One was fragrant with the aromatic scent of the forest – earthy and fresh and shining with dew.

When we moved to the hills de Grood, our black Labrador dog and I used to walk the trails and at the bottom of the property where the tree-ferns grew was a burrow in the bank that fascinated Groody – he was in a fervour of excitement whenever we were in the area and try as he might, the entrance that led to the dark mysterious cavern was too small for him to wriggle through. Frustrated, he forsook his quest and bounded through the ferns and bushes to find me.

But that did not stop Groody thinking about him. He wondered what lived there. The scent that emanated from somewhere below and beyond his reach, was unlike anything he knew, and it excited him to a frenzy. I had been told about a wombat that lived there now here he was, he had come to visit me. Groody was away following his own pursuits which allowed me time to tempt Little One with food. I offered him bread and milk, dog food, bits of meat and cheese but he regarded me with disdain and shuffled off into the realms of the eucalypts.

A naturalist lived nearby. He told me that wombats were root eaters.

"Try chopping up some raw vegetables," he said.

That was the solution! I also learnt that this small friendly animal, with squat legs and stocky body was nocturnal, which is why we had not seen him on our rambles.

The children all enjoyed the cottage and sometimes they would take their girl friends, or boy friends. They cut logs for the fire, lopped trees, cleared the fallen branches. Graham and I went to the Hill Nursery and bought azaleas which we planted in amongst the native bushes and trees. But my first project on taking possession was the fireplace. The whole of one wall was bricked over and the fireplace was a transformation.

≈ ≈ ≈ ≈ ≈ ≈ ≈

One day I was in the garden when Groody became alert. I looked up and saw a man walking towards me. As he came down the drive I noticed he was tall, neatly dressed and a stranger to me.

After an initial growl de Grood wagged his tail. I trusted Groody's instinct and invited the stranger in as I was about to put the kettle on. We chatted over a cup of tea. He said he was a new immigrant, looking for a place to live. He said he did not like big cities. He had a wife and four children. He questioned me about the schools in the neighbourhood and I told him all I knew. He sounded well educated and did not mention his profession. I enjoyed our brief encounter and as he was leaving I told him I looked forward to becoming acquainted with his wife.

Not long afterwards there was an accident. His wife was driving and one of his children was killed. This appeared in all the morning papers, together with a photograph of my visitor. The man I had entertained was none other than Ronald Biggs, the notorious and infamous train robber. My immediate reaction was one of shock. I rang the local police. They arrived quickly and after questioning me they set off with tracker dogs and a helicopter flew low for several days but

Sunday, September 28, 1997   The Province.

TREATY THREATENS GREAT TRAIN ROBBER'S RETIREMENT:

RIO DE JANEIRO — The aging Englishman laughs at the idea of visiting Britain.

"I keep reading that I'm pining for the green, green grass of home," says Great Train Robber Ronald Biggs, 68. "All I have to go back to is a prison cell, after all. Only a fool would want to return."

But Biggs may have little choice. In August, Brazil and Britain ratified an extradition treaty.

Though Scotland Yard has not yet asked Brazil to hand over the fugitive, British prosecutors want Biggs to finish serving a 30-year sentence for 1963's "great train robbery."

Biggs was one of 17 robbers who stole $10 million Cdn from the Glasgow-to-London Royal Mail Train.

One of the 12 gang members who were caught and convicted, Biggs went over the jail wall in 1965 and just kept going.

Police would eventually find Biggs in Rio but, without an extradition treaty, they were powerless to take him back.

When Brazil considered deporting him, Biggs produced another surprise — a Brazilian girlfriend pregnant with his child.

By law, Biggs could not be expelled as long as his son Michael, a Brazilian citizen,

was his dependent. Even so, Biggs' early life in Rio was no paradise.

With no passport or work permit, reporting twice a week to the police, Biggs eked out a living by doing odd jobs until the Christmas Eve that a reporter asked for an interview and agreed to pay a few hundred dollars. Virtually broke, the fugitive discovered he could make a living just being Ronald Biggs, "gentleman bandit."

Biggs could scarcely believe it. "I thought I must have been nuts not to do it sooner."

Meanwhile, his son grew into a child-star. As part of the kiddie singing group Balao Magico, he had a hit TV show and sold eight million records.

His son's earnings helped buy a roomy, terraced apartment high in Rio's green hills.

And Biggs' celebrity status made him a tourist attraction. For $90, visitors can enjoy a barbecue at the Biggs home, listen to tales of the heist from the man himself and buy a T-shirt that read: "I went to Rio and met Ronnie Biggs ... honest."

Biggs tackled other quasi-jobs. He recorded with the punk-rock group Sex Pistols, wrote a memoir called Odd Man Out, even promoted a home alarm system with the

'All I have to go back to is a prison cell, after all'

AP photo

Together with his dog Blitz, Ronald Biggs enjoys 'the simple life' in Rio de Janeiro.

slogan: "Call the thief."

Then, in 1995, Brazil and England final-ly signed an extradition treaty, although it would take two years to ratify. Bigg's son was 21 and no longer in school and depen-dent. Suddenly, the safety net was gone. Still, Biggs' lawyer insists he has nothing

to worry about since Brazilian law does not permit extradition once the 20-year statute of limitations for robbery has expired.

"I live simply," Biggs says, his face florid from the tropical sun and a fondness for Antarctica beer. "I do enjoy life."

— Associated Press

Biggs escaped to Brazil, where he has lived in exile ever since.

After the Biggs affair another man came down the drive – a very different type of man and I was glad of Groody. He bared his teeth and rolled back his lip, a low growl rumbled within him and the hair on his back bristled. The man stopped. He shouted at the dog to buzz off. I asked him what he wanted as he began to walk towards me. He was an unsavoury look-ing character and I told him that if he did not get off my property I would set the dog on him. He took another look at Groody who was rearing to go and, shouting abuse at me he made a hasty retreat.

It was rumoured that vagrants roamed the hills and when I arrived at the cottage sometimes I had a strange feel-ing that someone had been inside. I discussed it with the neighbours who told that wanderers were prone to sleeping inside if they could get in. They were considered harmless, just looking for a place to doss down especially in the winter-time.

However, my most terrifying experience happened when de Grood was not with me. I was woken from a deep sleep. I heard footsteps coming down the drive. When he reached the cottage I heard the louver door slowly opening. I listened… my heart pounded, the telephone was at the far end of the room. I lay there too petrified to move.

He entered the lobby… I had forgotten to lock the door. He tried the inner door which mercifully I had locked. I waited, and listened to the sounds of scraping and supposed he had some instrument and he was trying to turn the lock. I wondered if it was all a terrifying dream, was it really happening. Then he mumbled something to himself before walking round the side of the cottage and as he passed the window I prayed he would not look in and see me lying there. I heard him take the path that led into the forest, then all sounds ceased. I lay there a while longer, fearing he would return, before getting up and closing the curtains. I liked them open as it enabled me to gaze into the night sky before going to sleep, but would I after this? When I was able to think clearly I concluded it must have been one of the vagrants. Maybe he had done it all before, maybe it was he who I felt had intruded. I never again went to the cottage without Groody, my dear, faithful companion. I rang Nick and was grateful when he arrived bringing with him a dead-bolt which he attached to the door, only then did I feel more secure.

☙ ☙ ☙ ☙ ☙ ☙ ☙

Not many people lived on the hill. Many of them were professionals escaping from the big city at the weekends. My nearest neighbours were a family of four. They walked their dogs and goats, all wore leashes and the goats had bells attached to their collars that reminded me of Switzerland when I was there many years ago, the sounds of the cowbells always resounding through the hills.

One day a young girl appeared at my door.

"I've lost my goat! Have you seen him?"

This beautiful child with long fair hair and blue eyes looked pleadingly at me. I had heard Groody barking, now I linked the two together.

"Can you hear my dog barking?" I asked her.

She nodded.

"I think he may have found your goat. Let's go and see."

She took my hand and skipped along beside me. She told me her name was Heidi. We followed the path that led to the creek and there we found both Groody, and the goat happily demolishing one of my bushes. I took off my belt, slipped it over the goat's head and we dragged the unwilling animal back along the trail. As we neared the top of the hill we saw standing there, with an amused smile, the child's father.

We introduced ourselves and while Heidi tried to tether the goat we went into the cottage and I put the kettle on. He laughed often and had unruly hair and a beard. Over a cup of coffee he told me he was a High School Teacher in Melbourne. He had met his wife at Melbourne University. She had immigrated from Scandinavia, "a fair haired lass from Denmark. As soon as I saw her, I fell hopelessly in love! Soon afterwards we were married in a little church in the Dandenong Ranges."

They were lovely neighbours, they had one son, Stephen, and Heidi.

Others on the hill were either retired or occupied themselves with their gardens and orchards. Some kept chickens that roamed freely, others grew flowers that they sold to the florist in Olinda, some were market gardeners.

I never tired of the hills or my cottage. Seven years later when my turn came to sell I thought of Nancy Cranstone – she had so loved the cottage that she wanted to like the person who would live there. I felt just as sentimental.

I advertised in the *Melbourne Age*. The telephone started ringing early. Many people came, some were serious, others just curious but when a young man flashed through from one end to the other saying, "It is a little gem," he was the buyer of my choice, he would love it as I had. A solicitor was brought in and the Contract of Sale signed and finalized.

My days in Australia were coming to an end. I would soon leave the country for Canada. I spent my last day there alone, roaming the property with Groody. He kept close beside me. Instinctively, I think he knew it was the end. We walked between the ferns, and tree-ferns spreading their fronds in a wide arc, creating a canopy overhead. We said goodbye to wombat. Butterflies danced in the evening light and crickets whirred in the undergrowth.

The air was soft and languid and warm and away to the west the sun peeped through the trees and sank behind the mountain – the evening hill sounds were about to begin and the night breeze whispered in the tall trees. Then, slowly the moon, as if to say farewell appeared in the night sky and the owls began to call joining together the magic of the hills with the euphony of all the sounds of the forest.

Part Three
Canada 1977–1996

TURNING POINT

It was September when we camped our way through the Rocky mountains.

The snow-line crept down the slopes and we had finished our evening meal. The squirrels and the chipmunks joined us and the occasional deer peeped shyly, with one leg poised, as though ready for flight.

We sat round the log fire for the last time, the flames and sparks leapt towards the stars, our hands cupped round our hot rums, the delicious sweet aroma lingered on the night air. Peace was everywhere. We did not speak, we did not want to break the silence or disturb the memories. It had been a holiday of consequence and I knew, one day, I would return.

That was when my turning point was born, but it did not become a reality until four years later, when I closed my door for the very last time.

Thus it came about that I left the heat of an Australian summer and arrived in Canada in the middle of winter. I flew into Vancouver on a cold dreary day. I was tired and emotionally spent.

It had been a long and tedious journey but after a good night's sleep I felt infused with the spirit of confidence – the content of my life was now dominated by what was, rather than by what had been, and there was no turning back.

JOURNEY OF DISCOVERY

&

*T*he day I left Australia it rained. A freak thunder-storm hit Melbourne closing Tullermarine, halting city traffic and flooding the roads. My family and friends braved the elements and joined me in my drive to the airport. As I turned and waved goodbye I felt sad not knowing when I would see any of them again.

With the formalities behind me I climbed aboard. Break-fast was served soon after take off and for a while I slept. We flew via Nadi and Honolulu and touched down in both coun-tries but saw little of either, other than the inside of the air-ports where we waited in selected areas, like cattle in a hold-ing pen, I thought.

We flew back in time and crossed the International date-line. As we neared Vancouver I looker through the window of the DC8 and viewed the mountains covered in snow and marvelled at the irresistible fascination that bound me to British Columbia.

My daughter was at the airport waiting for me. It was wonderful to see her. We collected my bags and drove to the Grosvenor Hotel in Vancouver where I slept off my jet lag. Vancouver I liked, it had everything – ocean, mountains and Stanley Park with its wildlife and walking trails. From there, we drove to Horseshoe Bay and took the ferry to Nanaimo on Vancouver Island. The sun streamed through the lounge windows as we plied our way through the Gulf Islands, adding light and shade to the already colourful scene.

We booked into the Daffodil Motel not far from the city centre. I liked Victoria, British Columbia's capital and likened it to Hobart in Tasmania, both cities have deep water harbours with quaint streets and shops, and I promised myself that I would return.

We explored the island by driving over mountain passes with scenic views of mountains and lakes. We parked the car near bays and coves and walked the sandy beaches: the sun shone and everywhere, and everything glowed.

After a few days we drove to Kamloops in the interior, and Ray took me shopping – she said I needed winterizing, in other words, I needed some warm clothes as Canada after Australia was indeed cold. So with longjohns, boots and a down filled parker I was ready for anything.

We drove to McLure, a small village in the mountains, and I had my first lesson in snow-shoeing. I disgraced myself by falling three times amid gales of mirth, but I mastered the art before the day was over. The forest was sheer magic, the virgin snow where no one had been before, animal footprints the only sign of life's existence and the silence... merely sounds of the swishing snow-shoes, and the murmur of the breeze in the trees.

But as time passed by I felt the need to move on. I returned to Vancouver Island and this was the beginning of my journey of discovery. I called at the offices of the Red Cross in Victoria and asked if they could use me.

"Oh, yes!" was the reply.

"I need food. I need a roof over my head, and I need it now!"

I was given my first job. I commenced work the next day.

ONE MOONLIGHT NIGHT

⁊

*M*rs. Hind greeted me. She was going to England to visit her family and I was to care for her husband during her absence. Mrs. Hind showed me the rooms and where the medications were kept. She explained that her husband needed help with dressing and undressing, and showed me how to prepare his food. Then she left and I was on my own.

Albert was a big man, one of three brothers who were organ makers in days gone by. I soon discovered he could talk quite lucidly about the past, but could remember little of the present. He liked to talk about those days but his concentration was poor and he often lapsed into silence.

When it was time to prepare the evening meal he followed me into the kitchen and kept nuzzling me. I feared for his safety, that he might burn himself on the stove and suggested he looked at the television, but he refused unless I watched with him.

In the evening I gave him his sleeping tablet and we sat together until it was time for him to go to bed. I helped him undress and left a low light burning on his bedside table, then I too, went to bed.

Bert was incontinent and wet his bed each morning. When I asked him why he did it, he said, somewhat shamefacedly, "I can't undo my belt."

We discussed the problem and he agreed to leave off his pyjama pants. He watched me fold them and put them in a drawer beside his bed and if he wanted them he knew where to find them.

Bert's bed remained dry for three days, then he had a relapse. I suppose Sigmund Freud would have had an explanation. But as morning after morning I carried his wet bed linen to the laundry I wondered if it was a deliberate ruse to get my attention.

On one occasion I sat down to write when the telephone rang. I left my letters with my writing pad on the table. When I returned they were missing. When I asked him what he had done with my letters he looked blankly at me and either couldn't, or wouldn't reply.

Later, one of my uniforms disappeared. Where he put my things I do not know. But he knew. When his wife returned he produced them and gave them to her.

One night I awoke and lay listening, but could hear nothing. I don't know what woke me. I was not conscious of any sound. I crept to his room. His bed was empty.

"Dear God," I said aloud. "Where are you?"

Panic seized me. Collecting my robe and slippers I searched the halls and lobby but he was nowhere in the building. I dashed back for the keys before going outside and saw him trotting up the road of Oak Bay.

It was a night of glorious moonlight. I trod the dusty road softly so as not to disturb the deep slumbers of the world.

When I reached him I slipped my arm through his, saying, "Where are you going at this hour of the night?"

Bert shook my arm off impatiently.

"She has gone away with another man and I am going to find her."

I took his arm firmly.

"It is dark, we won't be able to see her tonight. Let's go home and I will help you find her in the morning."

Bert became docile as I turned him round and arm-in-arm we began the slow walk home. But as we turned I was horrified to see a police car coming towards us. I did some deep breathing and hoped we would be spirited away, that some miracle would render us invisible, but it was not to be. The car slowed to a halt and the policeman asked, while looking quizzically at the pantless man beside me, "Is everything alright?"

"Yes," I replied, "everything is fine and we are nearly home."

Declining his offer of a lift, we continued on our way. Once inside the building I felt relieved and helped him up the stairs and put him to bed like a child, the child he had become. He should have been in a home but his wife could not bring herself to put him there, although, I doubt he would have known the difference.

INTO THE UNKNOWN

⁊

*W*hen I left the Hind establishment the Red Cross sent me to care for a Jewish lady and I learnt the art of Kosher cooking.

Having accomplished two short jobs and gained some experience I left Victoria for Vancouver. The train became my chosen mode of travel. Pat and Petra came to see me off at Vancouver's Main Station and as the train pulled away I watched them growing smaller and smaller, until they faded into the distance. Suddenly I felt very alone. It was an emotion that washed over my like a wave.

A porter showed me to my small compartment. My bed that doubled as a sofa by day was comfortable with clean white linen. For a few minutes I gazed through the window at the passing scene – the Indian Reserve, some dilapidated houses, rain splashed windows. I shuddered and pulled down the blind to shut out the gloom.

A host of thoughts crowded my mind: Recollections of leaving my father when I left England. Memories of my last day in Australia. Now Canada, and I wondered what physical or spiritual challenges lay ahead of me.

I looked in the mirror beside the tiny wash basin. What a wind-swept vision appeared before me! I tidied my hair and used some lipstick. The train gathered speed as I swayed my way along the corridor to the restaurant-car. I was shown to a table with two other travellers who were visiting from Europe. They spoke little English and conversation was stilted but we shared a bottle of wine and laughed at each others misunderstandings. I enjoyed Canadian salmon, followed by strawberry mousse, and after coffee I returned to my roomette.

Clambering into my bed I quickly became accustomed to the motion of the train and fell asleep. In the morning I raised the blind and peeped through the window – the rain had ceased, the clouds had blown away and the sun shone. Here was a new day, a new beginning and my spirits soared. I quickly dressed and returned to the dining-car.

I was about to sit down when a lady came through the door and walked towards me.

"May I join you?"

"Please do," I said.

We soon got into conversation as she told me about her daughter who lived in Toronto and she was on her way to visit her.

"What about you, where are you going?"

"Toronto," I replied, "to seek my fortune."

And we both laughed. We introduced ourselves. Donna, I liked. I was glad of her company; she was cheerful and her happiness was infectious.

Donna told me her home was in Brentwood Bay, on Vancouver Island and when I visited her sometime later I discovered she was a very talented artist. In the middle of her main room a spiral staircase led to her studio, a circular tower overlooked the bay, the yacht club and mountains and most of her paintings reflected the scenic beauty surrounding her.

We left the dining car and climbed to the observation coach and as we neared Jasper, with cameras clicking, we observed the panoramic splendour of the landscape. We watched as a silver fox streaked by like a graceful gazelle, and a herd of deer stood still, filled with curiosity as the train moved slowly past.

Three days later, the train pulled into the station disgorging its passengers, a dishevelled looking lot. There was a numbness in the air as people scrambled for their luggage and walked purposefully towards the exit, the only sounds were the tapping of the womens' heels and the slamming of carriage doors. Donna raised her hand in a gesture of farewell and vanished in the crowd. Lost and bewildered my search for a porter proved fruitless. I dragged my bags to the taxi rank and waited in the queue. The YWCA was to be my temporary home.

Toronto was a big and impersonal city. From the top of the Sky Dome, I viewed the skyscrapers, Provincial Parliament Buildings, its huge shopping complex, and the sandy peninsula jutting into the lake that helped to form the natural harbour. And the people! Why were they all in such a hurry I wondered.

The aroma of coffee lured me and a cappuccino restored me. I bought *The Globe and Mail*, Toronto's main daily news paper, and studied the job vacancies and read the following –

Housekeeper: light housework, plain cooking, mature, nature loving person, abstainer, drivers' licence, Uxbridge area.

My International Drivers Licence proved useful. I applied and was accepted.

THE STRANGE LADY

❦

*T*he interview took place in Mrs. Duc's town home in Rosedale, an exclusive suburb of Toronto. She explained that her country home was miles from anywhere and hidden away in hundreds of acres of pine forest.

"If you feel like joining me the job is yours. Do you drive?" she said without a pause.

"Yes," I replied but I did not tell her that I had not driven on the other side of the road.

After much preparation the time came for us to leave and I found myself the chauffeuse of a Lincoln Continental. We packed everything into the car including the two black Labrador retriever dogs, and set off.

Driving through the city was a nightmare for me and Mrs. Duc had to guide me and I was more than relieved when we hit the open highway – there my tension ebbed slowly away and I was able to enjoy the scenic countryside. Uxbridge was a small village with tree-lined streets and old established homes with beautiful gardens. This was where we would shop for food, and collect our mail and newspapers. In the middle of the village was a pond with rushes and Mallard ducks, a peaceful setting that reminded me of some of the English hamlets I had known as a child.

Continuing our journey we turned on to a gravel road until we came to a gate that led to a track in the forest, and to "Frogsmere" in the middle of nowhere, just as Mrs. Duc had explained to me.

Mrs. Duc's residence was no country cottage but a palatial two storey home. It was utterly remote and as the weeks passed the last of the snow vanished, young growth welled up and over the grass lay a film of delicate green. There were fruit trees and vegetables that the gardeners looked after and everything grew and flourished with astonishing speed. There was no television, only a little transistor radio to keep us in touch with the outside world.

Frogsmere was surrounded by wide verandahs and as the weather became warmer we planted tubs of fuchsias, petunias and other herbaceous plants and we enjoyed some of our meals together on the porch amid the blossoms. But she was obsessed with the past and her broken marriage.

"I fell in love when I was very young," she said. "He was Swiss. We married and had one daughter. He left me for another woman and returned to Switzerland, taking with him his new bride. I could not forgive him. That was when I invested in this property and built Frogsmere. Here, I can escape from people and the world of disillusionment. People think I am a recluse and they are right, that is exactly what I am," she said dramatically.

Mrs. Duc could be charming but her moods swung like a pendulum and I did not know from one day to the next what to expect. She would pace about shouting at the dogs, or the gardeners, or me! The dogs would cower and with ears down and tails between their legs they sought my companionship and we wandered off for long walks in the forest, and by the time we returned her anger had dissipated and peace reigned.

One of her foibles was to shut herself behind locked doors and listen to the classics for hours at a time. Sometimes I sat on the porch with the dogs and listened, and to the accompaniment of the frogs that lived in a nearby pond. Sitting there as dusk began to fall I watched the shadows of the trees spread tracery over the sloping lawns that tumbled into the lake below. How lovely it could all have been.

But her bad temper finally got the better of her. Some irresistible impulse made her go to the tool shed. She stomped off to the flower garden and thrust her spade into the soil. I watched fascinated. Almost immediately she cried out for help. I rushed to her assistance but was unable to move her. Seeking the help of one of the gardeners we half-dragged, half-carried her indoors and up the stairs to her room. With difficulty I helped her undress and into bed. I suggested calling the local doctor but with a withering look at me she snapped, "the local doctors are no good!"

I was in a quandary. I bought her an electric blanket for comfort and carried her meals upstairs and listened to her perpetual moans. It became an intolerable situation. Finally, she demanded to be taken back to Toronto. I put dust sheets over the furniture in preparation for our departure, packed her belongings and mine and put them in the Lincoln. Mrs. Duc was in a great deal of pain but Rick, one of the gardeners managed to settle her comfortably in the car.

As we drove along I could see she was suffering and suggested, "maybe we should call into the Women's Hospital for advice when we reach Toronto." (She had already rejected the suggestion of an ambulance.)

To my relief, she agreed.

On arrival she was put in a wheelchair. At her request I went with her. Tests showed a cracked rib, probably caused when she thrust the spade into the soil. I stayed in the Rosedale home with the dogs until Ruth, Mrs. Duc's daughter, arrived before returning to the YWCA.

The following day remained hot and sultry. Nearby was a park with a stream winding deviously to I knew not where. I sat beside the creek and listened to the sounds of the water babbling and to the distant hum of cars on the freeway. It was peaceful there and my mind slipped into the past, to the place where I was born, the marshes, the streams that surrounded our small village. I don't know how long I slept I was only aware of the perfume pervading the air. The linden trees lining the water's edge were in full bloom and murmurous with bees as they fluttered lazily from one blossom to another. I wandered on, and by the time I reached the YWCA, I knew what I would do… I wanted to see Ottawa.

OTTAWA

I took the subway to Union Station and caught the early morning train.

I liked everything about Ottawa. It was a lovely city, the weather was a contributing factor, the sun shone continuously but it was not humid like Toronto, and on the train I met Bruce. He had lived in Ottawa for most of his life and was proud of his birth-place. He took me on a tour of the city, the fine parks, embassies and gardens, museum, and a conducted tour of the Houses of Parliament. We wandered around the art gallery together, there we met Mrs. Lester, a friend of Bruce's.

She asked me what I was doing in Ottawa and when I told her I was working my way across Canada, she said, "you are the very person we are looking for. Friends of mine are going overseas, they need a housesitter. Would you be interested?"

"Oh, yes," I replied. I could not believe my good fortune.

I was introduced to Stefan and Marie, a Polish couple who had emigrated to Canada before the outbreak of World War II and they were going to Warsaw to be reunited with family and friends whom they had not seen for many years.

Their home was on the outskirts of the city. In addition to their home with its Persian rugs, paintings and antiques, there was a cat, and a dog, a golden labrador named Toby. Two days later I moved in.

There was little for me to do apart from feeding the animals. Bruce continued to see me and to take me sightseeing. It was Queen Victoria who proclaimed Ottawa the Capital of Canada in 1857. The Dutch Royal family spent their enforced exile in Ottawa during the war, and as a token of their appreciation the Dutch people sent over millions of tulip bulbs.

"Now, each year there is a festival when the parks and gardens are a veritable wonderland. Perhaps you can see it sometime," Bruce said.

Bruce described how the Ottawa River froze in the winter, how cold it was and how people skated, some even skated to work.

I enjoyed myself housesitting and used to get up early while there was still some dew on the grass and walked through the garden to the orchard, Toby bounding along beside me. It was a spiritually uplifting start to the day.

One morning the dog seemed particularly excited, he bounded ahead, then back to me. He did this several times until we reached the shed. I looked inside, curious by all the barking and excitement, and low and behold, the cat had given birth to a family of kittens. Toby followed me everywhere and watched as I carried bowls of milk, water and food to Mother cat.

I would like to have stayed longer but six weeks later when Stefan and Marie returned I had to move on. Bruce drove me to the station. I will always remember Bruce with gratitude because without him none of my Ottawa experiences would have happened.

And I missed Toby, always there beside me.

CHRISTMAS IN NOVA SCOTIA

*

$\mathcal{I}$ caught the 11:30 night train. I slept, but fitfully. As we neared Nova Scotia the sky glowed red and the sun peeped through the early morning mist. The taxi wound its way along the sleepy city streets to the sound of the fog-horn and I booked into the Chateau Halifax. After a hot bath I fell into bed and slept deeply until the alarm woke me. With a sense of excitement I made my way to the restaurant and enjoyed brunch – ham and eggs, fries, toast and coffee.

It was not light enough to see much of Halifax from the windows of the taxi but what I saw I liked. I went to the lobby to book one more night but, to my chagrin they were fully booked and the clerk said, "I don't think you will get in anywhere, a world-wide fishing conference has flooded the small city."

She suggested I try the "Y", but that too, was fully booked.

I bought a copy of the *Halifax Chronicle* and returned to my room somewhat chastened by this unexpected turn of events. Hastily I read the advertisements. Two jobs presented themselves; one with children that had already been taken, and the other a long distance call.

The voice on the end of the line sounded pleasant, saying, "I will send my son to interview you."

We met in the lobby of the hotel and after a drink he took me to dinner. I had not enjoyed an interview with dinner before and found it a very pleasant experience. I remember wearing a black slack suit with fitted jacket, and a pink and grey paisley chiffon blouse.

John, my benefactor, was an architect, his father a doctor, and his mother in hospital having suffered a stroke and it would be my job to care for her if I decided to stay. The wine flowed through me and I felt warmth for this young man who had so trustingly accepted me on behalf of his father.

The following day we drove to Bridgewater, a little fishing village in Nova Scotia and I was taken to the local hospital to meet Isabel. We had an immediate rapport. The task ahead was not going to be easy but I felt that together, we would succeed.

The doctor I met later. He was a semi-retired physician who had delivered most of the village children. They worked by barter – he took care of their minor ills and the people brought gifts of chicken, fruit and vegetables. He was a kindly gentleman who enjoyed a good book and a game of chess in his spare time.

They lived in a century-old timber home and I had a complete suite on the top floor overlooking the garden that was large and neglected. Until Isabel came home, having little to do, I cleared the weeds and found rose bushes together with delphiniums and a host of other perennials struggling to reach the sun. I persuaded the doctor to take me to a nearby nursery and we bought a variety of annuals and with care everything flourished and soon produced a colourful array of flowers. Ben was most impressed! He was no gardener but he arranged for a young lad from the village to cut the lawns.

When Isabel finally returned her face shone with happiness.

"What a welcome!" she exclaimed. "I am so happy to be home and I have never seen the garden look more beautiful."

Isabel was an artist and there were water colours and oils all over the house, pictures of seascapes and landscapes, birdlife, and rugged fishermen with their nets and trawlers – she had captured the spirit on canvas in all its many moods and her sketches, too, were graphic.

Nova Scotia was an artists' paradise with its many coves and rural countryside, expansive views of picturesque lighthouses that jutted out on to the headlands. In the sunshine it presented a colourful scene but when the relentless, bitter Atlantic storms roared with savage velocity, nothing could have been more desolate and I marvelled at the courage of the lighthouse keepers.

Isabel progressed slowly. I took her for walks in her wheel-chair but she tired readily. During the warm summer days we often sat in the rose-garden and enjoyed the peace, the gentle hum of the bees and the subtle perfume of the blossoms. She often thought about her early life and what it was like growing up in a small community in Nova Scotia. Her father wanted her to be a musician but her greatest joy was painting and sketching, then she broke down and wept wondering if she would ever be able to paint again.

We both enjoyed music and spent many happy hours together listening to her favourite recordings. I read to her and took her to the local library to choose her own books and the days passed as imperceptibly as time itself, from summer and into autumn when the trees turned crimson and gold and displayed all the richness of fall.

The long summer evenings grew shorter and a chill descended upon us before the snow clouds gathered and the first flurries began to swirl through the air. Isabel grew restless. It was too cold to take her for walks. The physiotherapist came regularly but progress was slow.

Ben and I spent long hours discussing the problem until one morning I had an idea. Hurriedly I went to him.

"Ben, an idea has just occurred to me: you have a beautiful home filled with paintings, Isabel's paintings. Why not exhibit them? Let the people come."

Ben did not reply immediately, then he said, "I think it is a great idea, let's discuss it with Isabel."

We sat together round the table and we put the proposition before her. She was so excited she wanted to start preparing right away. We drew up a list of people who would be invited and sent them to family and friends as far away as Halifax, and to everyone in the local community. Soon the house was filled with enthusiasm and excitement and Isabel found new meaning in living.

As the time drew near we decorated the home with holly and lit the fires. Ben took care of the cocktails and I, the savouries. When the day arrived we wheeled Isabel in to mingle with the guests.

She wore a pale blue dress, long to hide the brace on her leg.The hairdresser had called during the morning and her fair hair, flecked with silver, shone like a halo. Fortunately her stroke had not affected her appearance and her speech very little. It was a festive occasion and Isabel loved it. She sold some paintings, and everyone radiated the warmth of love and happiness for her.

With the departure of the last of the guests we went into dinner. During the summer months there were flowers from the garden, and food served at table with wine, but with the coming of Christmas there were candles and holly for decoration. That evening Ben ate heartily but Isabel, buoyed with excitement, had little appetite.

When the meal was over we returned to the lounge and sat together round the fire. We watched the sparks disappear into the chimney and listened to the friendly crackle of the logs while outside the snowflakes continued to tumble, numbing the sounds of the passing cars and the distant songs of praise of the carollers. We were all reluctant to leave the comfort of the fireside but with the warm glow of the dying embers still upon us we took Isabel to her room and helped her to bed. She was happy. We turned down the light and kissed her goodnight. As we left the room I turned and looked at her – she was at peace.

Ben and I enjoyed a final nightcap and a game of cribbage before we, too, retired. Ben put the guard to the fire, and I fed the cat. The day was complete.

Before going to my room I went in to see if Isabel needed anything. She was surrounded by an aura of tranquillity. But as I looked at her, I became afraid, and crept closer. I listened, but could hear nothing. Nothing but the ticking of the clock on her bedside table. Tears sprang to my eyes as I realized I had lost the Isabel I had grown to love.

☙ ☙ ☙ ☙ ☙ ☙ ☙

Some months later I arrived in Banff and found Deer Lodge, an alpine chalet in the mountains and joined a group of hikers. Each day we climbed the trails and enjoyed the intoxicating scent of the damp soil and crushed leaves. The exhilaration of the fresh clear air lifted me spiritually. In the evenings we sat round the log fire and talked about our lives, our hopes and expectations. Here, I found peace.

I thought about Ben. I cared for him. When Isabel died he was a lonely man, lost for a while in his grief. There was nothing for me to do, my job had ended but I stayed for a few months to help him over a difficult period. Ben taught me to play chess, and I encouraged him to walk. Each day we wandered to the cemetery. It was not a morbid desire, it was wild and untamed with maple trees and natural woodlands. Ben used to like to sit beside a pond and reflect, and theorize about life, between its beginning or its end and the present.

When the snow disappeared and spring returned I began to think about moving on. The longer I stayed, the more Ben relied on me. We went to a concert in Halifax to celebrate his birthday. We dined in a little place down on the waterfront. The wine, good food and the atmosphere warmed us, followed by the music of Mozart and Vivaldi. When we arrived home I felt the time had come for me to break the news of my imminent departure but I could not destroy his happiness. I waited until we had finished breakfast the following day. I didn't want to leave him, but I knew I had to.

"Ben, I have something to tell you."

"I think I know what you are going to say. I have been expecting it... please, don't go."

Poor Ben!

Ben drove me to the bus station. He looked a forlorn figure standing there beside his car. The emotional strain of the past few months was too much for him and he wept as he watched the bus turn the corner and pull away.

LIFE IS BUT A GAME OF CHANCE

⁊he time came for me to leave Banff. Rejuvenated, I flew back to Vancouver. As I was about to disembark I was surprised when an arm reached over and picked up my overnight bag from the seat beside me. A man asked where I was going. As I had no plans, I said, I didn't know, but thought I would go to White Rock. He said he would take me as he lived there, "that's assuming you would like the ride." He had been golfing his way around Canada, so he said.

It all sounded too improbable but as he was putting my bags into the trunk of his car I could see clubs and other paraphernalia pertaining to his activities. Surreptitiously, I summed him up and decided life was after all, a game of chance.

When we reached White Rock we looked for somewhere for me to stay and found a motel with kitchenette. It was elevated and overlooked the water. Then he left and I did not see him again. To this day I do not know who he was, only that he had been my good Samaritan who lived in Crescent Beach nearby.

The motel was pleasantly situated in a garden setting, the rooms large and light. I hung my clothes in the cupboard and made a cup of tea. Refreshed, I wandered down a steep slope towards the waterfront and found a corner store where

I purchased some provisions and a local paper before climbing back to my room with a view.

Reading the news and scanning the advertisements I found the following notice:

> *Middle aged gentleman planning motor trip across*
> *Canada and return this summer seeks lady compan-*
> *ion, non-smoker, slim, medium height, who enjoys*
> *travel, camping, interesting conversation.*

I telephoned! We met! We walked, and we talked about ourselves and our lives, and discovered we had many mutual interests that promised well for two strangers planning such an excursion together.

We studied books and maps culminating in a regulated plan and on the fourth day of July we set off on our across-Canada journey.

Bob, I found to be an excellent companion, an Agricultural Scientist working with Canadian University Students Overseas (CUSO). There was so much I wanted to know about Canada, the wildlife, fauna and flora, the prairies and crops and Bob knew it all.

I would not describe it as one of the most comfortable periods of my life because we slept in sleeping bags on the ground in a tent, and I was so cold. But it was an experience. At night, after supper which I cooked while Bob set up the tent, we sat round the camp-fire and drank hot rums. We reminisced and listened to music, and very often to the hauntingly beautiful cry of the loons – a sound that aroused strong emotions in me, a sound I will never forget.

On our third day we reached Alberta and pitched tent in the Waterton Lakes National Park. In my diary I wrote 'it was the coldest night of my life!' It was pouring with rain and in the middle of the night the tent blew down. I fled to the shelter of the car. My emotions were at low ebb and I wondered how I could have undertaken such a foolhardy adventure, but in the morning I knew my journey had only just begun – the early morning sun rising above the mountains glistening with new snow and reflecting in the lakes was wondrous. Never in my entire life had I experienced anything so spiritually uplifting. The loons were silenced but the finches sang in the bushes nearby, as clear and sweet as the translucent morning air.

We piled the wet tent and everything else into the car and set off for Cypress Hill Provincial Park in the middle of the prairies. It seemed incongruous that in this vast, treeless tract of land, we would find a lovely campsite amidst a forest of whispering aspens, the trees filled with yellow wild canaries that fluttered about like leaves on the wind.

We drove through prairie country passing cattle ranches, corn granaries and oil fields. In Manitoba we passed through rolling country and many acres of golden mustard, blue flax and sunflowers. We visited Regina, the capital of Saskatchewan, and wandered round the legislative buildings, museum and university, and Wascana Lake. On the fourteenth day of July we drove beside Lake Erie to the spectacular Niagara Falls. Two weeks, and and four-and-a-half thousand kilometers later we reached Montreal, in Quebec.

We stayed with Bob's daughter, Barbara, and John her husband. They lived in an old home in Westmount. After dinner we climbed Mount Royal, which is the most striking feature of Montreal. It rises in the centre of the city and from the summit has an expansive view of the narrow streets and quaint, historic architecture that reminded me of a stage that had been set, waiting for the play to begin.

It had been a long day but finally we were shown to our room and after sleeping on the ground for two weeks, a bed offered welcome comfort.

The following day the four of us drove to Lake Massawippi, north of Hatley, and stayed in John's cottage on the cliff-top overlooking the lake. The cottage was tucked away in acres of forest and the beach with its warm white sand was ours, and ours alone. The trees ran down to the water's edge and provided shade from the hot noonday sun.

We swam every day and went snorkelling and sailing – snorkelling enabled us to explore the strange, often beautiful world beneath the surface of the lake. And at night when the moon was full, swathed in towels we scrambled down the cliff trails before stepping into the silken caress of the still water.

Lake Massawippi was a solitary place, an escape from the city, a place to dream and reflect, our only visitors the squirrels and racoons that scrounged for food. I'm glad I met Bob without him none of this would have been possible.

Bob and I had been living a carefree and nomadic life but suddenly time was running out. Bob had to return to Vancouver to prepare for his next expedition, this time to Ghana in Africa. We packed our belongings into the car, bade farewell to Barbara and John and set off.

Once again we hit the road. We camped from one camp-site to another until we reached beautiful British Columbia. Seeing the mountains I felt I had returned home.

Bob and I had travelled countless miles and enjoyed scenic and climatic variables, from the colourful prairies with endless crops of golden grain, interspersed with fields of chicory that looked as though a little bit of blue sky had fallen from heaven to the hikes through the rolling hills and mountains. But the time of day we loved most was sitting round the log fire under the stars, savouring our hot rums before turning in for the night when the world around us became quiet and intimate.

THE NAKED BODY

&

I had worked my way from the Pacific to the Atlantic and had lived out of a suitcase for a long time. I began to yearn for a place I could call home. Bob had gone off to Ghana and my temporary abode was the YWCA in Vancouver. My search began in the West End: It was a brilliantly cold and sunny day as I explored some of the sidewalks, and as I walked along Robson Street I noticed a vacancy sign for a one bed-room suite. I skipped down the five steps that led to the entrance and buzzed the manager. He took me to the tenth floor – the rooms were large with an unbroken view of the water-front. I was completely captivated. I paid my deposit, signed the agreement and left walking on air and the sun shone more brightly than ever.

The day I moved in the sun continued to shine. While I awaited the carriers I placed everything in my mind's eye and as I unpacked my china, sliver and paintings they were like old friends that I had not seen for a long time.

I had resided there for a little over a year and was well established when I arrived home one day to find a body out-side my door. I rang the manager. His language! I thought I had heard everything during the war, but the torrent of ob-scene words left me aghast! The manager prodded the man

with his foot. There was no response. The bawdy language
began all over again as he dragged him back to his room and
flung him on his bed where he left him. Red with rage the
manager mumbled something to me and departed. Then there
was peace.

I picked up the telephone and rang a friend. "Pat, you
will never believe what I am about to tell you. I have just
returned from a walk and outside my door, curled up in the
foetal position was my neighbour, absolutely starkers!"

"Do you mean he had nothing on?"

"Yes," I replied, and we both laughed.

I made a cup of coffee and went through the glass sliding doors to the balcony. Christopher, my pet gull flew low
and landed on the railing. I found some bits of chicken in the
refrigerator and he took them from my hand. Christopher had
come to me soon after I moved into my apartment. He was a
large Glaucous gull, snow-white with pale grey wings and
pink feet and legs. I sat back in my chair and looked admiringly
at him. My eyes wandered over the tops of the trees to the
water, the cruise ship passing by and the mountains beyond.
How beautiful it all was and how fortunate that I had found
such a glorious location.

A chill breeze ruffled Christopher's feathers. I went inside for a cardigan and as I was putting it on I thought of my
neighbour lying there. I crept into his room. Unwashed china,
food left over from the previous meal cluttered the table. I
shivered at the sight, covered him with a blanket and left,
closing the door behind me.

I did not see or hear my neighbour for days. During
that time other things happened to distract me. I was walk-

ing. It was a glorious spring day, one of those days when it was good to be alive. I heard a bird singing. Looking up into the tree I saw a finch and did not see the pitfall just ahead of me. I tripped and fell. How stupid one feels! Two elderly ladies enjoying the sunshine saw me, and rushed to my assistance.

"Are you hurt?" they anxiously enquired.

"No," I lied, and wished they would go away. After some superficial conversation I continued my walk and felt my shirt sleeve getting tighter.

By the time I reached home my arm was painful and swollen and although a few days later the swelling had subsided, an ugly purple lump remained. I sought the help of a doctor who lanced it, bound it and sent me home. But during the night the bandages slipped. I searched for dressings without success. I knew no one in the building. I thought of my neighbour. I pulled on my robe and wrapped my arm in a towel and rapped on his door.

"Do you mind the sight of blood?" I asked.

"I was in the navy during the war, I have seen my share of it."

I introduced myself and explained what had happened.

"I'm Paul," he said. "Won't you come in?"

He took my good arm and led me to a chair. While Paul looked for some dressings I glanced at the transformation. His room was spotless! The windows wide open, and the view across the yacht-club and mountains shone in the morning sunshine. There were table and chairs on the balcony. He had evidentially been enjoying his breakfast when I interrupted him. Could this be the same man I had found in a drunken stupor?

Later that day, close to dinnertime, there was a tap on my door. It was Paul. In his hands he held a tray with a covered plate. He carried it to the kitchen, saying, "I thought this would help!" Then he left. There was roast pork, crisp golden potatoes, carrots, peas, and cauliflower in a cheese sauce. This astonishing man, so kind, so pitiful when he had been drinking.

Some weeks later I found a little note under my door. "Joan, will you join me for a drink this evening? Come about eight o'clock. – Paul."

It was September. We sat on the balcony. I wondered why he had invited me. I asked him about his early life and that opened a flood of conversation. He was born in Quebec and educated there. He loved to travel and was in France in 1938, the year that I was there so that gave us a common interest as we swapped experiences and recollections. In 1939 he left France for England and joined the Royal Navy.

Life continued quietly for a while, until one evening hammering on my door Paul shouted, "Joan, call the police, he's got a butchers knife, he's going to kill me."

Hearing the urgency in his voice, I did as he bade me. Almost immediately six policemen arrived – two stationed themselves in my hall, two by the exit, and two went into Paul's' room. There was a scuffle. The policemen brought out a young man in hand-cuffs. Then they left as quietly as they had arrived and I went back to bed.

But the night was not over. Again Paul came to my door. He seemed agitated.

"My telephone is out of order, will you report it?"

"Paul, it is 3 o'clock in the morning. Let's get some sleep. I will call them later."

When I went to his apartment I found the cord on the telephone had been severed. Paul had not noticed and was devastated.

"Joan," he murmured, "you are the only friend I have."

I felt compassion for this unhappy man and answered nothing, for what was there to say.

Paul was a tall, distinguished looking gentleman with blue eyes and when he was sober I could not have wished for a better neighbour. I doubt he remembered the incident that brought us so unceremoniously together. Few people in the building would have anything to do with him, some of them left because of him, while others gossiped and cast judgement and aspersions upon him.

Vancouver was my home. The view from my window was ever changing. The cruise ships continued to sail past. There was Stanley Park, the Lost Lagoon and the bird sanctuary, Beaver Lake, mountains and forest trails.

Never would I find a more beautiful location and I was not going to allow Paul to drive me away.

SPRING, IN THE AUTUMN OF LIFE

❧

$\mathscr{I}$ helped Freddie into his wheel-chair and pushed him into the garden. The azaleas and rhododendrons were in bloom; it was a lovely day. The blue sky with whisps of white clouds scudded away into the distance, the swiftly flowing water of the canyon rushed headlong towards the ocean, the constant accompaniment to the song of the robins. Winter had passed.

We found our sequoia tree. It was a favourite haunt of ours. I adjusted Freddie's pillows, covered his legs with a rug and kissed him lightly. Throwing some cushions onto the grass I used the buttressed trunk of the old tree for a backrest, and enjoyed the fragrant scent of cedar. In my pocket I had a diary...

I began to read:

> *We met in the bank. There was the usual lineup.*
> *In front of me was a tall fair man and as the*
> *queue moved slowly I became curious. He had*
> *fine physique. Was he good-looking? How old*
> *was he? Those were the questions turning over*
> *in my mind. As if by telepathy, he turned and*
> *smiled at me. I smiled back. We talked about the*
> *slowly moving people ahead of us, the weather,*

*and other inconsequential snippets of conversa-
tion, and as we neared the tellers he smiled and
said, 'Let's have some coffee together?' I nodded
in silent assent.*

   *When the tellers had finished with us we
walked to a nearby cafe. We found a seat by the
window overlooking English Bay and watched
the yachts with their white sails dancing in the
wind. There was a stiff breeze and the water
choppy. A perfect day for sailing.*

   'Would you like to be out there?' he said.

   'Oh, yes,' I replied.

   *'I had a boat once, but that was a long time
ago, when I lived in South Africa,' he said. Then
he spoke about his early life in Holland where he
grew up on his father's farm, the war years in
England, followed by a few years in Cape Town
before finally settling in Canada.*

   *We prepared to leave the cafe when he
stopped and looked at me.*

   'I don't know your name,' he said.

   *'I don't know yours either,' I replied, and we
both laughed. We introduced ourselves and left
the restaurant hand-in-hand.*

Freddie had an appointment and I wandered home. A
chance encounter had suddenly brought this man into my
life. Was he married, I wondered, would he call me as he said
he would?

   The evening dragged on and my mind was like a grasshopper flitting from one flower to another, not settling for long on anything and when the sun sank behind the mountains leaving a crimson glow across the water, I began to prepare for bed. I was about to slip between the sheets when the telephone startled me into consciousness.

Hearing Freddie's voice I felt the strain of anticipation ebb slowly away as I snuggled down between the bedclothes. I was happy and at peace with myself.

& & & & & & &

The telephone rang early. I, barely awake was surprised to hear Freddie's voice.

"It's a glorious morning! Will you join me for a walk?"

"I would love to," I said.

We walked along Vancouver's waterfront. Few people had left their beds and all was still.

We watched a bald eagle swoop into the water and make a sudden attack on a fish and fly with it into the distance. And noticed a young mole, lost, and almost blind, unable to find his way across the path. We picked him up and held his little warm furry body and laid him gently on a mound of fresh soil and hoped he would be able to find his way underground.

As we walked along the seawall, Freddie talked to me and all the questions that had been floating around in my head were answered: his wife had died after a prolonged illness. He had two children and four grandsons.

When we reached the Tea House we stopped for breakfast. We ate outside in the garden under the blue and white striped umbrellas overlooking the ocean, and watched the freighters coming and going to we knew not where. It was as Freddie had said 'a glorious morning', and the beginning of a beautiful friendship. We walked often, went to concerts, dined and danced, and Freddie taught me to play golf.

We spent many happy holidays together touring Vancouver Island and the Oregon Coast. But one of our happiest vacations was spent hiking the Cariboo and Chilcotin country in the centre of British Columbia.

FAR FROM THE MADDING CROWD

&

$\mathcal{F}$reddie and I prepared for our departure and left Vancouver early. Four hundred miles lay ahead of us. We spent one night at 100 Mile House before continuing our journey along a gravel road to Nimpo Lake where we joined our guide and a group of active seniors in search of adventure. The sun was setting across the lake, it was dusk and the loons were calling to one another. Our cabin overlooked the lake; there was a pot-bellied stove in the corner of the room with the wood waiting for the strike of a match. It was wild but comfortable and we were instantly endeared to the place. This was Nimpo Lake in the heart of the Cariboo country.

We tossed our bags into our cabin and hurried through the woods to the main building for dinner and were met with old-fashioned hospitality, home-made bread fresh from the oven and trout from the lake. Two fires were burning one at each end of the cabin. There were book-shelves on all the walls: wherever there was a space there were books, novels, reference books, books on fishing and trapping, others telling us about the local area, what to do and where to go and how to do it, and there were easy chairs set around the fires for our enjoyment at the end of the day.

After a good night's sleep we set off on our tour of

exploration. Our only means of travel was by plane. Near our cabin was a floating dock made of wood that jutted out into the lake. We flew in a little Cessna or a lumbering Beaver from one lake to another and then hiked. We had packs on our backs and cameras slung around our necks.

There was something magical about flying in a tiny plane over lakes and mountains into the early morning sunrise. The plane seemed flimsy as we rattled our way through the air to Turner Lake – deep, and placid as a pond.

We followed trails leading up to the Hunlen Falls. The morning mist kept swirling through the canyon mixing with the spray and the roar of the water cascading into the Atnarko River before plunging into Lonesome Lake hundreds of feet below. Peace was everywhere with only the sounds of crackling twigs underfoot and the occasional chatter of squirrels. There was a profusion of wild flowers, coloured and varied toadstools and ferns, but the highlight of the climb was when a grizzly appeared as if from nowhere and shuffled into the bushes nearby.

We flew over the Monarch icefields to Bella Coola viewing lakes which from above looked like blue jewels interspersed with snow and ice. Bella Coola lay in a valley of incomparable beauty surrounded by almost vertical walls of mountains. Norwegians were the first white settlers, the fjords of the surrounding area reminded them of their native Norway and this is what endeared it to them. Bella Coola was a modern community where Indians and whites lived in relative harmony side-by-side in fishing and forestry. The village consisted of general stores and a post office, churches of all denominations and the Cedar Inn where we stayed and shared our room with a little mouse that came in through the window.

From there we flew with Wilderness Airlines to Ocean Falls, a small logging and fishing village. It was wild and isolated, the terrain so rough the only access routes were by sea and air. Few people live there now but at the turn of the century it was the beginning of a prosperous little town that grew rapidly due to a successful pulp and lumber mill. The community throve until the Provincial Government bought the mill and soon afterwards declared the machinery obsolete and inadequate, and subsequently closed it.

Ocean Falls has a very wet climate and the people who live there now are known as the 'rain people.' But we were lucky – during the time that we were there the sun shone down upon us with a temperature of ninety degrees.

Where houses once stood the debris had been cleared leaving carpets of flowers, an artistry of pinks and lilacs of the self-sown stocks. What caused Ocean Falls demise remains uncertain. Maybe it was due to the mill closing, maybe the winter snow-slides that rumbled down the mountains burying homes and apartment blocks causing many deaths. Who is to know? What a story it could tell if only the ghosts of the past could speak.

Last, but not least, we climbed through rain forests to see the Indian petroglyphs, said to be over one thousand years old. We had an Indian guide who scampered from rock to rock like a mountain goat. We were less agile but we all reached our goal.

Nimpo Lake, Bella Coola, and Ocean Falls remain haunting memories. The Cariboo's surreal landscape transcends the

rustic cabins and fishing camps. the scenery, a study in contrast from the blue-green lakes and sparse pines, breathtaking
rock canyons and river rapids, trout-filled lakes hidden amid
the rolling hills clustered by spruce and whispering aspens to
the peaks of the Rainbow Ranges, an astonishing spectrum of
reds, oranges, yellows and lavenders.

It was a holiday to remember! Far from the madding
crowd, no television, no telephone and no newspapers, just
the sounds of the loons, the scent of the forests and the intoxicating air of the High Cariboo country.

We said goodbye to our dear guide who had been kind-
ness itself helping us over the sometimes difficult terrain, and
bade adieu to all the adventuresome people we had enjoyed,
promising to write. Some of us kept that promise, others ...just
passing ships.

We drove to Hope and stopped at the Holiday Inn for
dinner. While we were enjoying our meal, Freddie said, "Let's
have one more night on the road?"

So we did. We lingered over our wine before walking
briefly through the sleepy little township and returning to the
Inn, and as we lay there in each other's arms, I wished it
could last for ever.

LIFE AND LOVE IN THE TWILIGHT YEARS

≈

*F*reddie was a Chartered Accountant and one of his clients owned a cabin near Jasper.

"You can use it any time you like," he told Freddie, but Freddie had never taken advantage of the offer because he did not like the idea of going alone and he knew no one who would enjoy, or understand the excitement and pleasure of roughing it in the wild, but when he asked me if I would like to go with him, I was thrilled.

Stocking up was half the fun! We bought candles, a supply of torch batteries, canned foods, sleeping bags, blankets and drinking water.

I had driven to Jasper many times and it was always a delight: crossing the Rockies a never to be forgotten experience of glorious panoramic views of perpetual mountains, snow and sunshine.

As we neared our destination the setting sun dipped and fell, while the moon appeared in the deepening clear, dark blue sky.

Freddie had no difficulty in finding the way. We drove along an unkempt track that led into the foothills. The log cabin was small with a wood stove. By this time there was scarcely light enough to see but with the aid of a torch, Freddie found wood for the fire and I unpacked the car. We lit the candles and lit the fire and in no time at all our little abode looked cosy.

Jim, the owner of the cabin, was a trapper and on the walls and floor were animal skins. Although my sympathy was with the animals the skins made a suitable decoration for the cabin and added some much needed warmth. The cabin had not been used for a long time and felt cold and smelt musty but the fire burned well and soon there was a gorgeous aroma of burning wood, and it was surprising how quickly the little room became snug and warm.

In one corner was a sink with an outside tap for water. Above the sink a window that overlooked the forest. And hidden amongst some trees nearby was the 'privy'.

I heated some Campbell's soup, there was bread and cheese, nuts and fruit and hot rums. The day was complete. We made up our sleeping bags in front of the fire and fell asleep.

☞ ☞ ☞ ☞ ☞ ☞ ☞

We awoke early, the sun shone, all was quiet, so quiet we could hear the silence. We donned our hiking boots and with cameras and walking sticks we wandered through the trees and hiked the trails. The forest seemed alive, the air stimulating, the scent of the firs and balsams, decaying leaves and damp soil pungent with mossy fragrance. We reached a clearing stretching before us. We came upon it unexpectedly and were bewitched by the beauty surrounding us. The woods ran in deep gullies and dropped precipitously into the valley below, the brightness of the snow magnified the shadows and enhanced the many shades and shapes of the conifers.

It was a glorious day; blue sky and not a cloud to be seen. As we stood there a strange sound echoed through the mountains and in a split second our silence was torn apart by an avalanche as a wall of snow roared down the mountain and into the valley below. Then there was silence. We watched mesmerized and were afraid. I shivered! Freddie put his arm round my shoulders and we quickly scrambled down the mountain leaving the eeriness behind. Once inside the cabin Freddie stoked up the fire while I made up a light lunch, and our world returned to normal. It had been a strange experience, one that we would not forget in a hurry.

After a brief rest we drove to Jasper village. Jasper is dominated by ice-capped mountains and great valleys, it is notable for its magnificent scenery and unique natural wonders. After taking the chair-lift to the top of Mount Whistler and viewing it all from above, we drove to almost seven thousand feet up into the snow country and ice-fields, we saw mountain sheep, mountain goats and a handsome bull elk. The Columbia Ice Fields is the longest of a chain of ice fields along the Great Divide. We viewed it from the Parkway, and then at close range by snowmobile, it presented a magnificent sight. The icefield covers a huge area, and is two to three thousand feet deep. It is formed by heavy accumulation of snow in the high mountain basins. Weight and surface melting compact the lower layers into solid ice.

We dined at the Columba Icefield Chalet at the foot of the glacier before returning to our little log cabin in the foothills. It had been a strenuous day. We sat by the fire enjoying our hot rums, then blew out the candles and slept.

☙ ☙ ☙ ☙ ☙ ☙ ☙

Another day of sight-seeing! I had been to Banff before: in September, the calm time of the year when summer was almost spent and the fall colourings were beginning to appear. Christmastime, when everywhere was smothered in snow and ice, coloured lights decorated the trees and bushes: And again in the spring. It was an artist's paradise in all its changing moods.

I liked the alpine village of Banff snuggled into the foothills of the Cascade Mountain. We parked the car and wandered up the main street with its gift shops of postcards, and knick-knacks that tourists like to buy, stores bulging with sports clothes, hiking boots and skiing equipment and found a little sidewalk cafe where we stopped for coffee and watched the passing people and general panorama. We took the gondola to the top of Sulphur Mountain and viewed Bow River and the Banff Springs Hotel, golf course, big horn sheep and mountain goats clinging to the cliff ledges.

We stopped at Nigel Creek Canyon and walked the trails to Peyto Lake. The scene was absolutely breathtaking – Peyto Lake, a brilliant emerald green, like so many lakes, fed by melting glaciers and surrounded by interminable mountain peaks of perpetual snow and ice.

We stopped at Melissa's Restaurant for dinner of the most delicious Alaskan crab legs. And when the day ended we relaxed by the fire and drank our usual hot rums and made love. What a day it had been!

❧ ❧ ❧ ❧ ❧ ❧ ❧

But all things come to an end as they surely must. This was our last day. We did not hurry up. Lying there in each other's arms, his body close to mine was sheer and absolute bliss. When we did bestir ourselves we were astonished to see two eyes looking at us through the window. Standing on hind legs, with front paws resting on the window-sill was a beautiful bear and in a tree nearby were two small cubs. We tried 'shooing' them away but they showed no fear. Freddie got two saucepan lids and started banging them together. The bear turned tail and bolted into the forest and one of the cubs scrambled down from the tree and rushed after her. But the second cub seemed too scared to move until Freddie thumped on the trunk of the tree, then he dropped to the ground and rushed off in the direction of the others.

We tidied the cabin and prepared to leave. It had been a glorious weekend but Freddie had to return to his clients, and I, to care for an elderly gentleman who had suffered a slight stroke – John McMaster.

It had been a holiday quite unlike anything either of us had experienced and it will remain forever etched in my memory.

❧ ❧ ❧ ❧ ❧ ❧ ❧

Freddie and I enjoyed other more leisurely times together, exploring the Gulf Islands where we stayed in comfortable Inns within easy walking distance of the beach, we swam, we played golf and always we enjoyed each other.

And as I re-read my diaries the memories all come flooding back. What began as a casual encounter in the Bank so long ago became the story of my life and love in the twilight years, the sort of romance that only dreams are made of. Maybe, it was destiny that shaped our lives! Who is to know? One thing is certain... our paths had not crossed in vain.

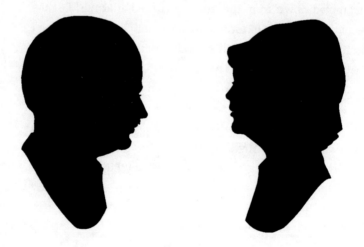

ISBN 155212512-2